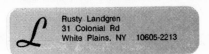
195 27
3.25

D1543318

Hetty Mooi

Creative work with textiles

VAN NOSTRAND REINHOLD COMPANY
NEW YORK   CINCINNATI   TORONTO   LONDON   MELBOURNE

Van Nostrand Reinhold Company
Regional Offices:
New York   Cincinnati   Chicago
Millbrae   Dallas

Photographs: Marijn ten Holt and
Ton Smeets
Illustrations: Hans Soet
Printed in Great Britain

First published 1972 by
Uitgeverij Cantecleer B.V., De Bilt,
Netherlands

Published in the United States of
America in 1975 by
Van Nostrand Reinhold Company
A Division of Litton Educational
Publishing, Inc. 450 West 33rd Street,
New York, N.Y. 10001

Library of Congress Cataloging in Publication Data

Mooi, Hetty.
  Creative work with textiles.

  Translation of Textiele werkvormen.
  Bibliography: p.
  1. Textile crafts. 2. Needlework. 3. Fancy
work. I. Title.
TT699.M6613 1975   746   74-29329
ISBN 0-442-25490-3

Contents

1 Experiment using different materials.
This mask was made from one square of cloth, and the object was to make sure that none of the material was wasted. Holes were cut in the material, and the cut out pieces used elsewhere in the mask. Pulling out threads was allowed, and all sorts of techniques could be employed as long as every scrap was utilized. In places the material was stretched, in others gathered, and wherever bumps appeared they were stuffed from the back with newspaper. The material, a coarse linen, was admirably suited for this design

Acknowledgement

The original idea of this book was based on the exhibition 'Studies in Textile' (Textielmuseum, Tilburg, January 1971). Thanks to the co-operation of the museum staff and the designers many beautiful photographs were taken which formed the starting point of this book. We should also like to thank the Algemene Vereniging van Docenten for all the information we received.

The illustrated designs were made by: Mrs Lenie Modderman, Mrs M G Kok, Sister Helena van der Berg, Mrs Damveld-Verswijveren, Mrs van Lammeren-Staal, Mrs Vroom-Maas, Carla Kamstra, Co Simons, Marian van Dijk, Marian Hilhorst, Sister Ferraria, Wilma Hoenselaar, Mrs Nellie Schrijvershof, Ans van Dillen, Miss Florantia Kool, Mrs Soeters-König, Jan Mooi, the pupils of St Bernardus, Amsterdam, Teachers Freeform Design, Application course MAVO, Den Haag, the pupils of De Scholengemeenschap in Stevensbeek, de Amstel MAVO, Amsterdam, the Kweekschool for Kleuterleidsters, Amsterdam, the pupils of the Montessorischool, Amsterdam, Saskia Veen, Helma Root, Carmen Kuiper, Karin Hamme, Marjet Knake, Taertske van Dijk, Willie Koopman, Heidy Vlees du Bois, Thea van Vliet, Yvonne van de Biezebos, Sandra Aertse Tuin, Liesbeth Bussing. All other designs were made by the author.

Marijn ten Holt took the photographs for figures 2, 4, 5, 7, 18, 19, 26, 35, 36, 44, 48, 53, 59, 63, 66, 67, 70, 71, 72, 74, 75, 77, 81, 82, 84, 88, 98, 99, 101, 103, 104, 106, 107, 108, 116 and colour plates 1, 2, 6 and 8.

Ton Smeets took the photographs for figures 9, 22, 43, 46, 47, 60, 65, 73, 86, 89, 110, 111, 112, 113, 115, 117 and colour plates 3, 4, 5 and 7.

The record office of the Royal Institute of the Tropics, Amsterdam gave the permission for the photograph in figure 54 to be reproduced; the Spanish National Bureau for Tourism in the Haque for the photograph in figure 64; and the photographic commission of the Rijksmuseum, Amsterdam for the photograph in figure 87.

Lastly, we should like to mention that the children's drawings in figure 62 were made by Philippe Huinck and Barbara Goos.

2 Woven material

3 Tabby weave

Fabrics

Work in any medium requires a certain amount of technical knowledge in order not to waste time attempting things which are impossible. For instance, a piece of wood cannot be bent over the knee, but a sheet of metal can; each material requires treatment suited to its inherent qualities. Therefore, before work in fabric is attempted, the basic qualities of the materials must be understood.

In daily life everyone comes into contact with textiles and acquires a certain amount of knowledge about them. For instance, one fabric may have a rough texture, one a smooth; one material is transparent, another opaque; one is loosely woven, another closely woven and firm. These facts have a practical application. For example, it would be a mistake to make a garment from a loosely woven fabric unless the garment were lined, but the same fabric would be quite suitable for curtains. Rough materials irritate the skin and are therefore more suited to outer garments or furnishings. Natural fibres such as silk, linen and wool are easier to manipulate than many synthetics, but also crease more easily and require more care in laundering.

To understand the nature and characteristics of different fabrics it is necessary to study the various methods by which they are made. These include weaving, knitting, crochet, braiding and knotting.

Weaving

Weaving is based on a two thread system. This can be seen by taking a piece of cloth and fraying it out, which reveals two sets of threads lying at right angles to each other. Space does not allow all the different methods of weaving to be described here, so tabby weaving has been taken as a simple example (figure 3).

A number of threads are stretched vertically on a loom to form the warp. The weft consists of horizontal threads woven in and out of the warp as shown in the diagram. The best way to understand the process is to make a sampler.

Hammer nails into two opposite ends of a flat-board or old picture frame and attach warp threads to these (figure 6). Then, using a thick needle with a large eye (a rug needle) weave the weft thread in at right angles to the warp in an under-over-under-over movement. Then introduce a variation such as weaving over two and under two, or over three and under three threads. With this method loose threads (known as 'floats') lie on the surface of the fabric, and materials such as huckaback towelling make deliberate use of this effect. Try introducing different coloured threads into the weft and note how this affects the composition by producing horizontal stripes. Experiment freely in this way to discover the possibilities of the medium.

There is another way of stretching a warp, without the use of nails. Take an oblong piece of formica, approximately 150 mm × 60 mm (6 in. × 2½ in.) and bind the rough edges with sticky tape. Alternatively, card may be used, but this does not stand up so well to the pressure put upon it. Stretch the warp round the formica in one continuous length, bending the formica into a curve as shown in figure 8. When all the warp on the hollow side of the formica has been woven the finished part can be moved round to the back and the weaving continued on the remainder of the warp.

Try using different types of materials for the weft threads, eg, grasses, reeds, drinking straws, nylon stockings, strips of cloth, twigs, etc.

For a description of more complicated weaving techniques, reference can be

4 Hand weaving using woollen
threads, nylon stockings, different
thicknesses of string and flax fibres

5 Weaving experiment, using a small horizontal table loom or simple hand-made loom of a board, with two rows of nails at opposite ends. Stretch a series of warp threads on the loom; these could be strong linen thread, as was used here, or fishermans thread. For the weft in this design, the weaver used cotton threads, thick and thin wool- *len yarns, bast, beads, drinking straws, pieces of wire, twigs and curtain rail*

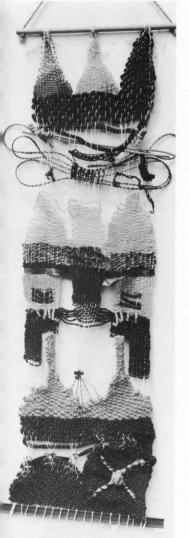

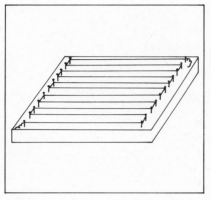

6 Simple loom

made to the bibliography at the end of this book.

Knitting

This is probably the most commonly practised craft, and by most people it is carried out automatically. It is a one thread system, worked on two needles. The required number of stitches are 'cast on' to one needle, in one of a number of different ways. After this the stitches are transferred from one needle to another in alternate rows until an area of cloth is built up (figure 10). As the stitches are looped into each other both horizontally and vertically, knitting stretches in both directions, a quality which distinguishes it from woven fabrics. It has other specific qualities which can be deliberately exploited. For instance, if a stitch is dropped, for whatever reason, then the stitches lying below it will drop too, forming a run. In creative knitting this can be used to form open patterns. Also, if a thread is pulled horizontally the knitted fabric will separate into two parts at that point. This can be useful for children's clothes which may need to be made larger as the child grows.

Crochet

Crochet is also a single thread system, but is worked with a hook. To 'cast on', a chain is made of the required length, using the fingers, or a crochet hook (figure 11). The second row is worked with the hook into these chain stitches, using one of a number of crochet stitches. These vary in height, the shortest being single crochet, then double crochet, half treble, treble, double treble, etc. By changing from one to another in one row, a wavy line is produced. This can be 'corrected' in the next row by working short stitches above the long ones in the previous row, and vice-versa.

Crocheting can be used for decorative edgings, especially on garments, and the chain has many uses; for instance as a weft thread, as a couched thread or for braiding. Because of the way the stitch is made crocheting is generally less pliable than knitting. In deciding on the relative advantages of crochet or knitting for making a garment much will depend on the yarn being used, the tension of the stitches and the particular garment being made. Knitting and crochet are easy techniques to learn, and help to teach co-ordination of the fingers, making them especially good exercises for children. Practice alone can produce even stitches, and the more skilled the worker becomes, the easier it is to improvise and create. The possibilities of knitting and crochet used creatively will be dealt with later in the book.

Braiding

Braiding (or plaiting) in its simplest form is based on a three thread system. It is not possible to make a braid with less than three strands (figure 12), but it is possible to use more (figure 13). To make the basic three strand plait lay the threads side by side, securing them at the

7 Sampler worked in darning on a waffle linen.
This has small floating loops on the surface which are linked up with embroidery thread to form the various motifs

8 Strip of formica with the warp wrapped round it

*9 This weaving experiment, worked
on the simple loom illustrated in
figure 6, used nylon stocking strips
and wool for the weft*

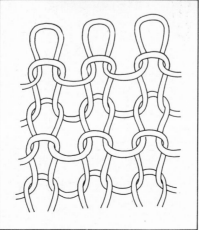

10 Knitting structure

top, and bring the left hand thread over the middle thread to the right, and the right hand thread over the middle to the left, alternatively. This can be done in a rhythmical manner, resulting in co-ordination of fingers and wrists. Braids can be made from wool, string, crocheted chains and strips of cloth with the raw edges turned in. The thread selected will determine whether the finished braid is flat or rounded in section. Braids can be used as a decorative edging on a garment or cushion, while a long braid can be wound round in a spiral and oversewn on the back to make a table mat or floor rug.

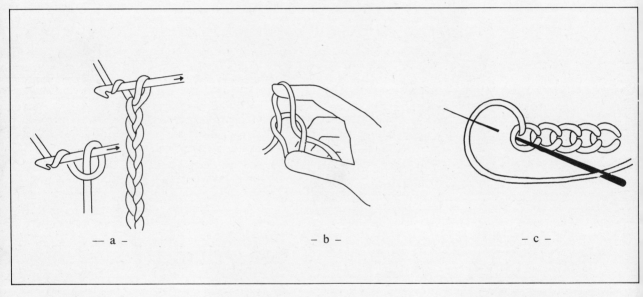

— a —   — b —   — c —

11 *Chainstitch*
a. *made with a crochet hook*
b. *made with the fingers*
c. *made with a needle as an embroidery stitch*

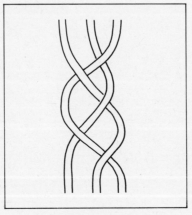

12 *Three strand braid*

13 *Six strand braid*

Egyptian Braiding
This technique, so called because it was used by the ancient Egyptians, requires a special loom, and is particularly suited to making large pieces of cloth. A braided fabric, like a knitted one, stretches in both directions, making it particularly suitable for clothing, and it was so used by the ancient Egyptians. A simple garment could be made by laying a number of braids side by side and oversewing them together on the back.

Knotting
One particular form of knotting, known as macramé, is at present very popular. Other types of knotting such as tatting and netting are not dealt with in this book.

Macramé is an ancient craft which originated in the Middle East. It was carried out originally on the spare warp ends when a piece of weaving was removed from the loom. It is used nowadays for a wide range of articles, varying greatly in scale. Fine work includes watch straps, jewelry, evening bags, collars and head bands; coarser string is used for shopping bags, flower pot holders and wall hangings and on a really big scale, hammocks, screens and room dividers can be produced.

Most macramé patterns are built up from a few simple basic knots, which are easily mastered. They are the square knot (also known as the flat knot or Solomon's knot), the half knot, the clove hitch (also known as cording), the half hitch and the Josephine knot (figures 14 to 17). (For detailed instructions, see the later chapter *Macramé*.) Macramé is worked vertically, from the top, but

14 a. The half knot (twist to the right)
b. The half knot (twist to the left)
c. The square knot (combination of (a) and (b))
15 Vertical clove hitch
16 Horizontal clove hitch
17 (a) and (b) Josephine knot (two stages)

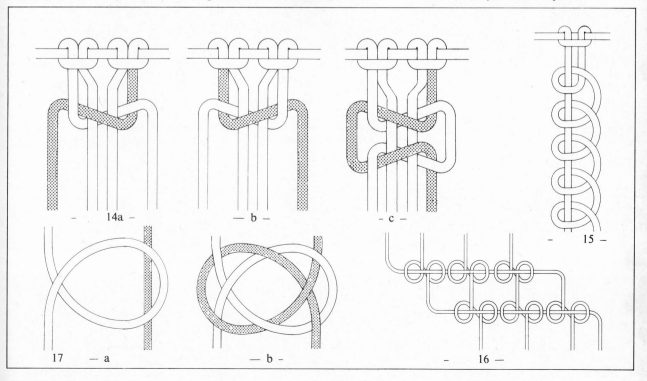

- 14a -   — b —   - c -   - 15 -

17   — a   — b -   - 16 —

18 Experiment with materials. The design on the left, was made by Mrs M Cr Kok. It is of flax fibres on a natural hessian (burlap) background with areas of drawn threads which complement and accentuate each other. The right hand illustration shows a weaving experiment by Helma Root: The hessian pieces were first soaked in glue, then put in place on a board covered with hessian, with beads added at random. More pieces were sewn on, and to add further interest, frayed and knotted threads

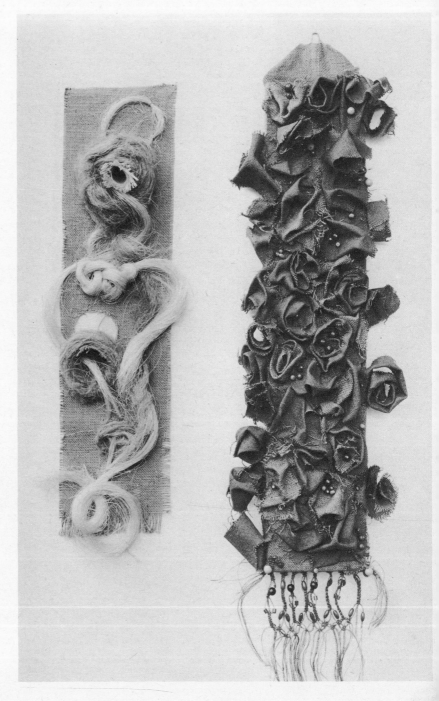

threads can be linked across horizontally to make a fabric. Beads can be incorporated to give added richness to the work. As with knitting and crochet, practice is needed to perfect the technique before moving on to the more creative aspect of knotting which is dealt with later in the book.

Having learned how to construct different kinds of fabric, profitable experiments could be made in cutting them up, learning to select the right kind of scissors for different materials, finding out which types of fabric can be torn along the warp or weft, what fabrics can be cut into fine pointed shapes, etc.

These pieces of cut and torn fabric, together with the crocheted chains, the scraps of knitting, the braids and the macramé samplers can now be put to some use. With a little imagination they can be used to build up a more complex sampler than anything hitherto attempted.

Try taking a piece of cloth as a backing and move all the pieces around on it until a satisfactory design is arrived at. This may be an abstract arrangement or a figurative subject suggested by the character of some of the materials. When the final form of the design is decided on the materials can be simply sewn to the background or carefully glued with a suitable adhesive.

Experiments with Threads
It is obvious that all cloth, whether it be knitted, woven, crocheted or knotted is composed of threads. The qualities of those threads, together with the means of construction, determine the characteristics of the cloth. It is therefore important to study the make-up of the threads used in order to understand their particular characteristics and behaviour.

Wool is for the most part spun mechanically nowadays, although some craftsmen still spin by hand. The advantages of the commercially spun yarns are that the threads are of a uniform thickness, and that they are strong even when very finely spun. In spinning the fibres of the wool, strands are twisted round each other forming one thread. Wool is especially suited to this method because each strand is made of scales, which, when twisted, grip each other, interlocking securely and making a strong thread.

Cotton fibres are without scales, but have a natural twist and when they are spun they twist around each other forming a long continuous thread.

Hessian is made of jute and because of its make up it goes limp, fades and attracts dust, but special finishes help to overcome these faults.

It is obvious that the characteristics of any particular thread affect the nature of the finished material made from it. If the thread is flimsy and a firm fabric is needed the thread can be used double, each pair of threads being treated as one.

By handling different kinds of threads, and experimenting with them, enough knowledge will be gained to make possible a really free approach to textile crafts.

Some threads are quite unsuitable for weaving. Amongst these are handsewing cottons, machine threads, embroidery silks, knitting, crochet and knotting yarns. They have their own characteristics which fit them to their particular purpose. Within each group of threads there is a wide range of thicknesses and textures, from which the designer can chose according to the nature of the project in hand. It is important to chose the right needle for a particular thread. Children must be taught to select the right size of needle or frustration will certainly follow. For instance, a small-

19 *Assorted threads*

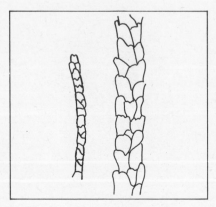

20 *Wool strands showing the scaley texture*

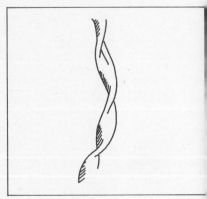

21 *The natural twist of cotton fibre*

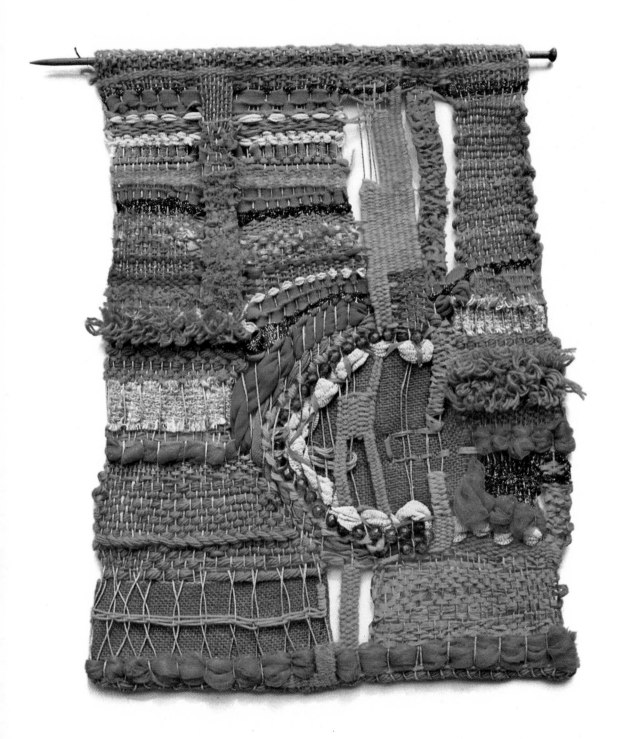

Colour plate 1 Weaving experiment using a nail board.
The main body of the design was woven in string, varied by thick and thin threads and old nylons, and added pieces of woven cloth

Colour plate 2 A frog worked in two tones of orange on a coarsely woven cloth, using traditional techniques in a free manner. These techniques were: drawn thread work, needle weaving, darning, Swiss, French and German embroidery. In the drawn thread areas, an overcast stitch and a spikey stitch, with darning technique were effectively used

22 *Pulled thread design sewn on to a linen background.*
First take a square of loosely woven linen, or scrim, machine sew a cotton strip all around, then fasten securely to a wooden frame. Pull out threads here and there. Distort the weave and enhance with embroidery stitches used freely. To finish, remove from the frame and sew on to a fabric background.

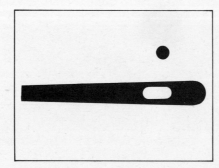

24 Designs constructed from circles
and squares

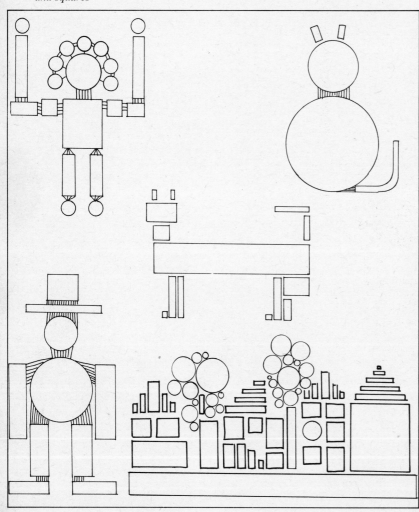

eyed needle should never be used for a
thick thread (figure 23) and when threading beads the size of the needle must not
exceed that of the hole in the smallest
bead.

The needle may be sharp or blunt
depending on the kind of fabric it must
penetrate. For example, on canvas and
loosely woven fabrics a blunt tapestry
needle can be used, but to pierce a close
weave a sharp point is needed. Crewel
needles, with long eyes, are suitable for
most embroidery threads, with chenille
needles for extra thick yarns and metal
threads.

Experiment by couching various types
of threads on to a fabric background,
arranging the threads in a pleasing design
and pinning them in place before begin-
ing to sew. Try also knitting or crocheting small rounds or squares to incorpor-
ate into the design.

It is a good idea if you are planning
to do this kind of work to make a col-
lection of materials. Save left over scraps
from dressmaking, cut up old clothes,
buy remnants and store them in boxes or
polythene bags grouped according to
colour or type of fabric.

Embroidery techniques

Probably the most popular type of embroidery is that of surface stitchery, usually worked on a smooth fabric such as a light or medium weight linen, using a variety of thicknesses of cotton threads. Crewel or chenille needles should be used, depending on the thickness of the thread, and the use of a thimble facilitates the work.

The design can be transferred to the fabric by the use of embroidery carbon paper (also known as tracing paper), by 'pouncing' or by ironing on a transfer. In counted thread embroidery, on the other hand, no design is put on to the material, which must be an even-weave linen, or canvas. Instead the design is worked out on graph paper which is used as a chart from which to count out the stitches during work. Counted thread embroidery includes drawn thread work, pulled fabric, cross stitch, Assisi embroidery. Hardanger work, black work and canvas work.

Stitches

The stitches used in surface embroidery fall loosely into groups such as flat stitches, looped stitches, knotted stitches, composite stitches and couching. Counted thread embroidery makes use of hemstitching, cross stitch, canvas stitches, pulled fabric stitches, etc.

Some stitches are common to both types of work.

25 Running stitch and variations

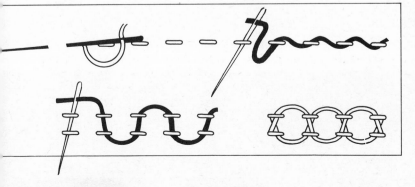

Running stitch

Pass the needle over the surface of the material, picking up a few threads at regular intervals so that the small stitches lying on the surface are all the same length, but somewhat longer than the spaces in between (figure 25). Several stitches may be taken on the needle before the thread is drawn through. To make a decorative border stitch thread a blunt needle with a contrasting thread and whip the running stitch. The tree in figure 26 is worked almost entirely in running stitch.

Back stitch

Bring the thread through fabric on the stitch line and make a small stitch backwards, bringing the needle out an equal distance in front (figure 27). Make another stitch back, inserting the needle at the point where it emerged the first time, and so on. (On an even weave fabric the threads could be counted and the movement would be back over, say, three threads, forward under six, back over three, etc.) Back stitch also can be threaded in an in-and-out movement or in a looped movement (Pekinese stitch).

Stem stitch

Work from left to right taking small regular slanting stitches along the line (figure 28). Keep the thread below the needle throughout the work. In cable stitch, which is a variation on stem stitch the position of the thread is alternated. Working from the left and with the thread *below* the needle, insert the needle a short distance along the line, bringing it out half way along the stitch formed. Repeat the movement, but with the thread *above* the needle and so on. This stitch is suitable for working on the counted thread.

26 Sampler of roughly woven cloth, with a tree design completely worked in running stitches, with french knots added to indicate leaves.

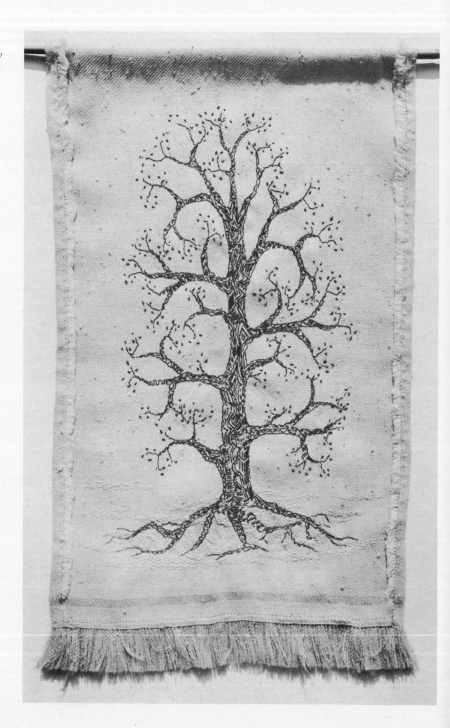

Herringbone stitch

Working from the left, bring the needle out on the lower line and insert it on the upper line a little to the right, taking a small stitch to the left, and with the thread below the needle (figure 29). Next, insert the needle on the lower line a little further to the right, making a stitch to the left and with the thread above the needle. Herringbone stitch can be varied by working the stitches close together or by whipping.

Satin stitch

Work straight stitches close together to fill any shape (figure 30). Blocks of stitches may be worked in different directions.

Blanket stitch

Blanket stitch is used as an edging stitch, for sewing down appliqué patches, and as a filling stitch (figure 31). Bring the thread out on the lower line and insert the needle on the upper line a little to the right, making a straight downward stitch, with the thread under the needle point. Pull up the loop and repeat the movement. There are many variations possible.

Arrowhead stitch

This consists of back stitches worked at angles to each other and can be used to build up geometric patterns (figure 32).

Chain stitch

Chain stitch can be used as a line or filling stitch (figure 34a). Working from the right, bring out the thread and hold it down under the thumb. Insert the needle where it last emerged and make a small stitch to the left, keeping the thread under the point of the needle. Pull up the loop and repeat the movement. Lazy daisy stitch, or detached chain is a varia-tion on the basic chain stitch in which each loop is anchored down separately with a small stitch (figure 34b).

Fly stitch

This is a variation on lazy daisy stitch in which the loop is left open at the top (figure 34c and d).

Cross stitch

Cross stitch is associated in many people's minds with the Victorian sampler, but it has many applications in present day life on clothes and household articles. Designs can be worked out on graph paper, each square representing one stitch; these are used as charts from which to count out the threads during work. It is essential to have an even-weave fabric with a well defined weave, or counting the threads becomes tedious and difficult. Cross stitch can be combined with Holbein stitch for Assisi work. In this the motifs are outlined with Holbein stitch and the entire background filled in in cross stitch, leaving the motifs 'void'. Holbein stitch is illustrated in figure 45. Cross stitch is also used on a background of alternate stem stitch (figure 37) in a type of imitation weaving. The basic cross stitch is shown with variations in figures 38 to 40.

Figures 43 and 44 show two samplers in which counted thread embroidery has been incorporated into a design. In figure 43 basic geometric shapes have been embellished with a variety of fillings, using thick and thin threads, and in figure 44 a formal arrangement has been built up, using variations on cross stitch.

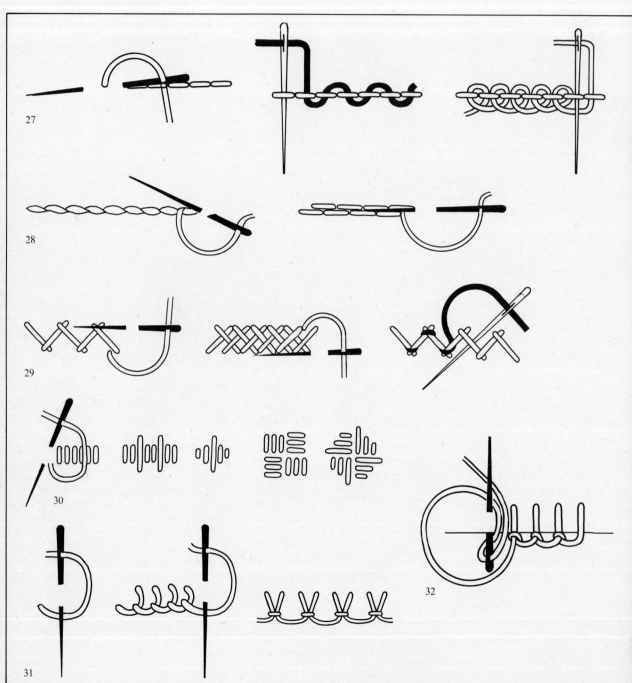

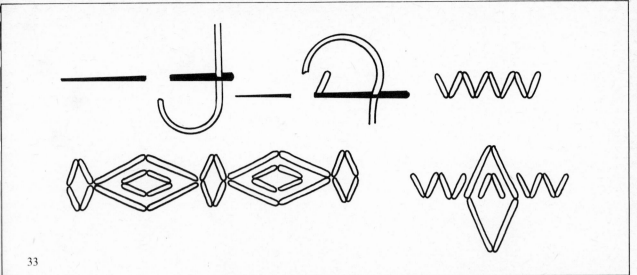

33

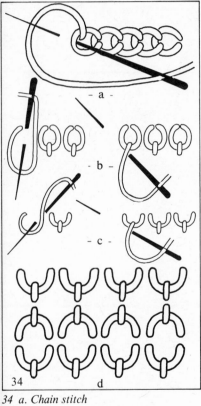

34

34 a. Chain stitch
b. Lazy daisy or detached chain
stitch
c. and d. Fly stitch

35 Dragon sampler using four em-
broidery stitches only, in bright
colours. Stitches used were arrow-
head stitch, blanket stitch, french
knots and back stitch in different
sizes

23

36 Close-up of the previous sampler clearly showing the background
cloth. With this type of material,
which is not suitable for counted
thread work, the embroidery stitches
must be worked in a free manner

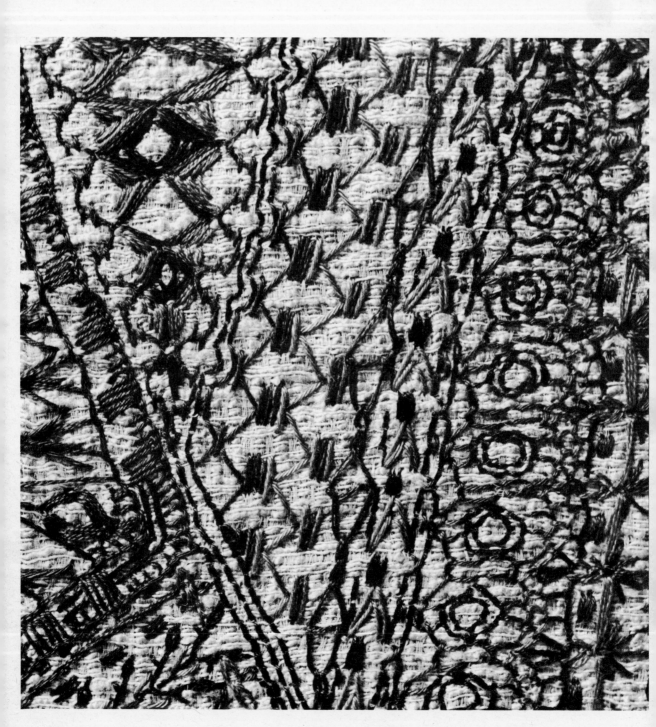

24

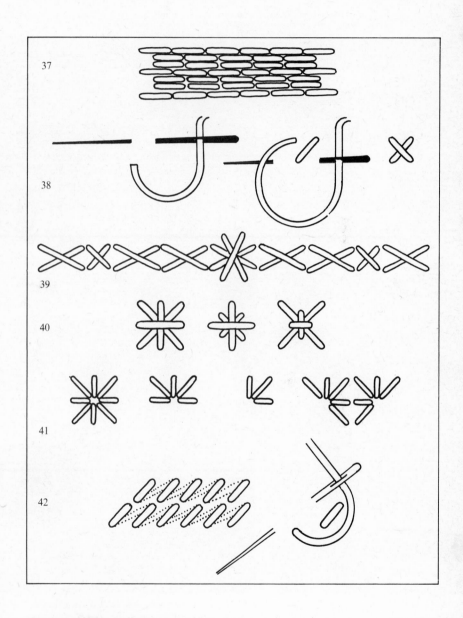

43 *Sampler showing geometric shapes filled with a variety of stitches and worked in threads of different thicknesses.*

44 *Cross stitch sampler in a formal geometric design, using variations of the cross stitch*

45 *Holbein stitch.*
This is based on two rows of running stitch superimposed on each other, the stitches in the second row of running filling in the spaces in the first row. The stitches and spaces in the first line must be of equal length

46 Black and white patchwork sampler, a group project.
Each person was given a black or a white square of linen, with a variety of thick and thin threads in the opposite colour, with instructions to create a 'picture' of spring, summer, autumn or winter. The stitches to be used were back stitch, satin stitch, chain stitch, running stitch and variations of these. When all the squares were finished, they were joined together to make one large wall hanging

Drawn fabric embroidery

47 Combination of drawn thread and pulled thread techniques. The background was of a coarse white material which is extremely suitable for drawn thread work, and darning techniques. It is imperative in this kind of embroidery to use a frame to which a piece of linen must be securely sewn before beginning work. To add more visual interest different thicknesses of yarn were used both for the darning techniques and the embroidery

In drawn fabric embroidery (also known as 'pulled work') groups of threads are drawn tightly together to form a lace like structure. The material should be an evenweave, but can be as fine as lawn or as coarse as sackcloth. The stitches used include satin stitch, cross stitch, eyelet holes and a whole range of specific drawn fabric stitches which can be found in any book on the subject. Designs can be formal, using the stitches as fillings for geometric or organic shapes, or can be very free, possibly combining drawn fabric work with other forms of embroidery as in the panel in figure 47.

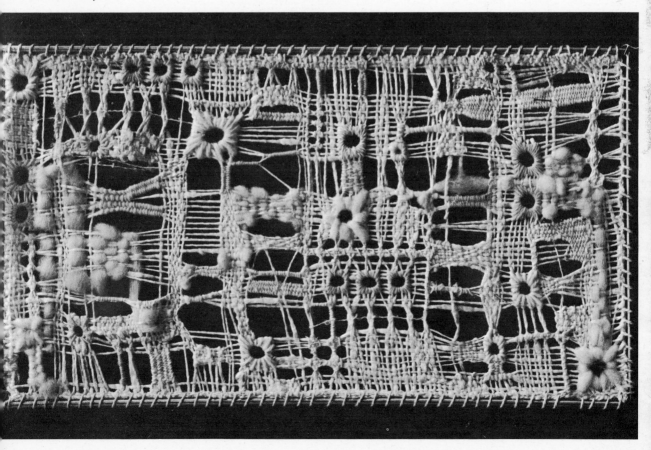

Drawn thread work

48 Design in white on a white
background.
*After stitching around the linen to
prevent fraying, holes were cut out
at random and embroidered around
in a similar manner to that of Swiss
embroidery, but using free shapes.
Techniques used were drawn thread
work, french knots and other surface stitches. The loops for hanging
the sampler were worked in needleweaving*

Unlike drawn fabric work in which the
weave is merely distorted, in drawn
thread work some warp and weft threads
are actually cut and drawn out of the
fabric. The remaining threads are tied
into bundles with hemstitching and
further embellished with threading,
twisting, needleweaving or by the introduction of contrasting threads into the
open areas. Surface stitchery can also be
combined with the drawn thread work.

Generally speaking all open work
techniques are more effective worked in
self colour as this emphasises the lace-
like quality of the work.

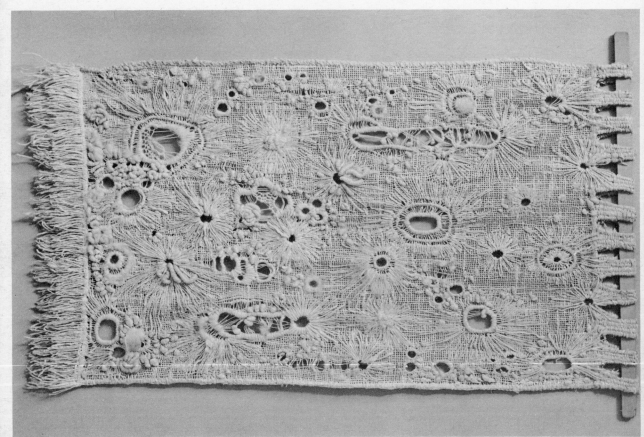

Designs on patterned fabrics

Patterned fabrics, whether printed or woven, can be enhanced by the addition of embroidery stitches. Gingham, for instance, is a woven fabric with light, medium and dark squares, and stitches in a matching or contrasting thread on some of the squares can alter the whole appearance of the fabric (figure 49). Stripes and spots too, lend themselves to further decoration with the addition of simple stitchery. The appearance of a stripe may be changed (figures 50 and 51) or spots linked to each other to form a new pattern, (figure 52).

49 Changing the appearance of gingham with stitches
50 Changing striped fabric with running and threaded running stitch
51 Stripes decorated with fly stitch

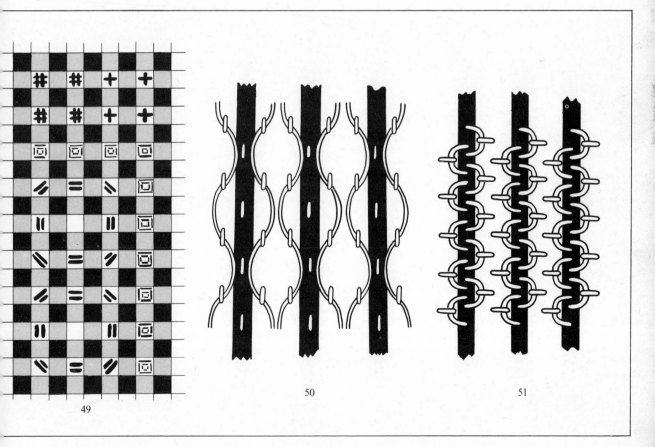

49

50

51

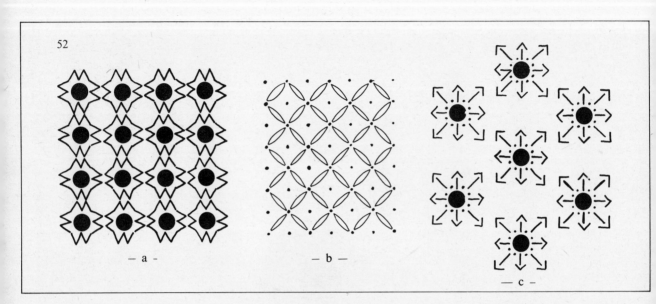

52

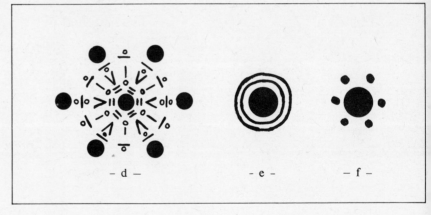

52 a.–d. Designs built up on polka dot fabric
e. and f. Emphasising individual spots

Colour plate 3 Wall hanging.
An example of machine appliqué
work combined with creative embroidery. The colours are harmon-
ous, and the picture is suitable for
a child's room

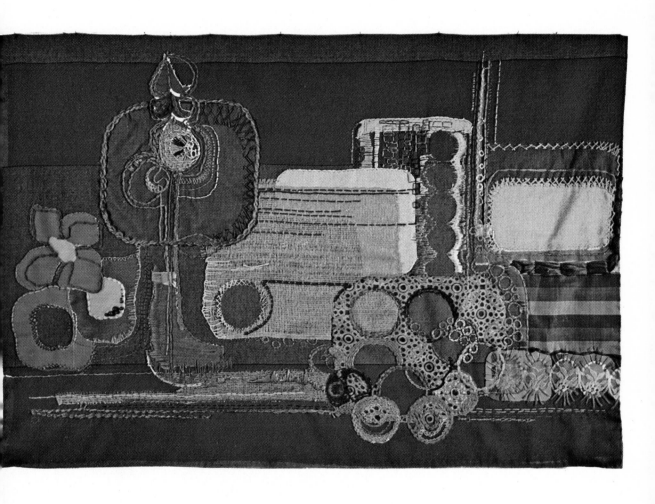

Colour plate 4 Wall hanging
Orange flower, *made in patchwork
using hexagon shapes.*
*An assortment of cotton scraps were
carefully chosen to harmonise, then
moved around until the final design
was decided upon. The pieces were
joined together with an overcast
stitch, the templates removed, and
the whole piece stitched onto a
backing*

Design

Looking

When contemplating any creative work it is important to look hard at things which surround one, both natural and man-made. A really close look at a tree, for instance, will bring home to the viewer how superficially he normally looks at natural forms. He knows that the tree has a trunk, branches and leaves, and he will recognise the general shape and characteristics of a particular tree, but to design from it he will need to look with far greater concentration to appreciate all the subtleties of form, colour and texture.

Try out the following exercise. Look closely at the leaves of a tree, noting the outside shape and the pattern of the veining within that shape; touch and appreciate the texture of the bark; study the changes of colour within an area. Now make a small sampler in any medium to bring out the character of some aspect of the tree which you have observed. Repeat the exercise with a stone, noting its overall shape, whether the surface is smooth or pitted like a crater. Find a suitable technique in which to convey your impressions. Man-made objects, too, can serve as a starting point for a design: for instance a wrought iron gate, the pattern of tiles on a roof or windows in a wall. The main thing is always to be aware of one's surroundings, making mental notes to be filed away for future reference.

The sense of touch plays an important part in all textile work and suitable materials must be found to convey the tactile quality of a particular subject. As an exercise, make a long crochet chain and experiment with it in relation to the 'tree' theme, drawing a linear design with it and sewing it down to a fabric background. After studying the tree work out your design from memory so that you do not slavishly copy the subject, but instead, make your interpretation which should bring out and accentuate its character. The crochet chain is not the only way, of course, of interpreting the tree and a whole series of different versions can be tried out using different materials and a variety of techniques. In this way knowledge is gradually built up of the possibilities and limitations of particular materials. Out of this grows a respect for the character of each material which enables ideas to be translated into fabric and thread in a sensitive and workable manner.

Colour

Returning to the study of a tree, much can be learned about the subtleties of colour. A tree trunk which at first seems to be just brown, will be seen, on closer inspection to contain a whole range of browns, greys, greens and purples. This is a point to bear in mind when interpreting the subject in a textile medium.

The colour of a piece of cloth may trigger off an idea for a design; for example a bright yellow fabric could inspire a design based on the sun or a sunflower. Colours have 'warmth' and 'coldness' and a warm colour such as red should not be used to express a cool theme. Blue, the coldest colour, gives a feeling of distance and is therefore suitable for suggesting horizons, sky and sea. Emotion can also be suggested by colour, red being associated with fiery passions, etc.

The grouping of colours in a satisfactory colour scheme is a complex problem. Some people have an inborn colour sense and instinctively use colour well. Others can be helped by theoretical knowledge, based on the colour circle (figure 61). Colours which lie next to each other in the circle will give harmonious colour schemes, while colours

*This is an imaginary creation made
in four steps. First invent a fantastic
word, then in your mind picture the
word as an object. Make a pictorial
representation of the object on
paper and finally make it up in
suitable materials*

which lie opposite each other give maximum contrasts.

Drawing
After an object has been looked at and touched, an attempt should be made to transfer the experience to paper (ie to make a design based on impressions gained while handling the object). This will not be easy at first, but a start can be made in quite a simple way and confidence will grow with practice.

Start by basing a design on the veining in a stone or the grain in a piece of wood. Although it may seem alarming at first, make the drawing boldly, say with a felt tip pen on a large piece of paper. Start in the centre of the paper with one firm, unbroken line. If this proves to be incorrect resist the temptation to start again, and put in the next line, and the next, until the drawing is complete. The original piece of wood or the stone serve only as a starting point and need not be copied slavishly. Keep your mind open to any chance effects which may be produced and learn to make use of them. At this stage an attempt could be made to work out the idea in fabric and thread, using a few simple stitches, but exploiting to the full the possibilities of design. The lines could be tried closer together, or further apart, but keeping in mind all the time the character of the subject.

As a more advanced exercise take, for example, a thistle, and try to convey in stitches not the actual appearance of the thistle, but the prickly feeling which it suggests. This will entail finding the right materials and searching for the most expressive stitches to convey the prickly sensation.

Another way of building up a design is to cut out a few simple geometric shapes, such as circles, and arrange them on a background, sewing them down when a satisfactory arrangement has been found by trial and error. A more complex pattern could then be evolved superimposing a linear pattern on the solid circular patches. Full use should be made of any chance effects which occur during the development of the work.

54 Detail of a batik cloth from Middle Java (copyright Royal Institute for the Tropics, Amsterdam). This is an example of how the viewer can put his own interpretation on a design. This could be seen as a bird with wings and feathers

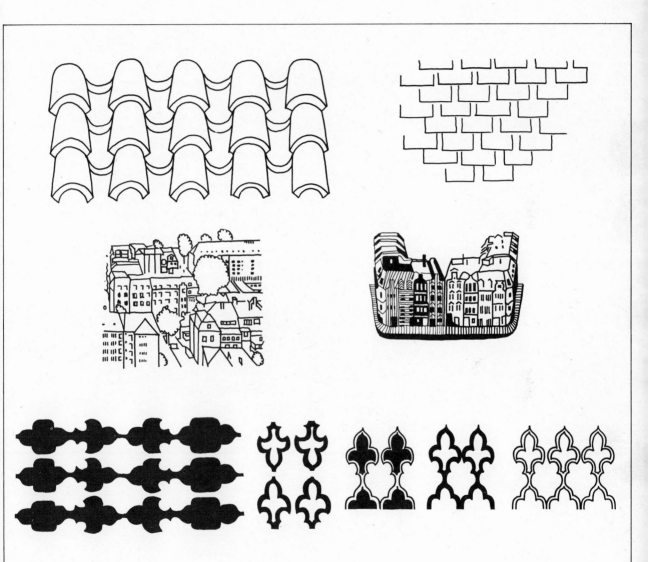

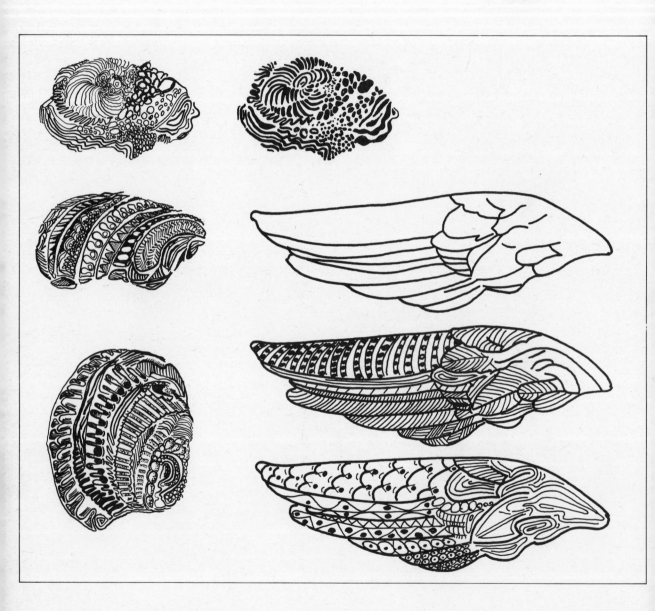

57 *Analytical drawings of lettuce,*
leaves, a papyrus flower and tiled
paths

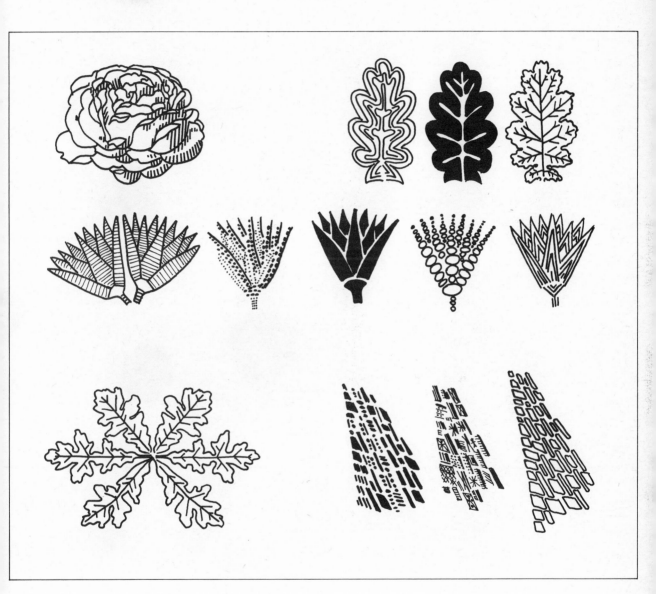

59 and 60 In this wall hanging a
Tjiwana motif was used as the
central theme. The Tjiwana is an
antelope-like figure which was
originally made of wood, and was
copied as a headdress for dancers of
the Bambara tribe in the Upper
Nigeria. The shape has been re-
peated in various ways with suitable
materials to suggest its African
origin

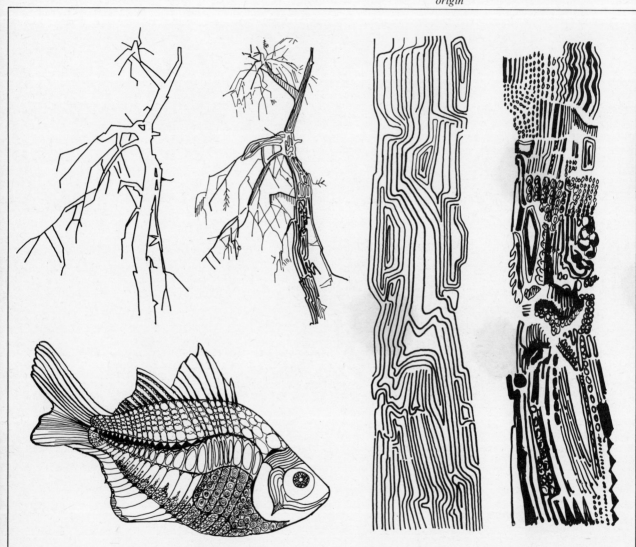

41

61 Colour circle

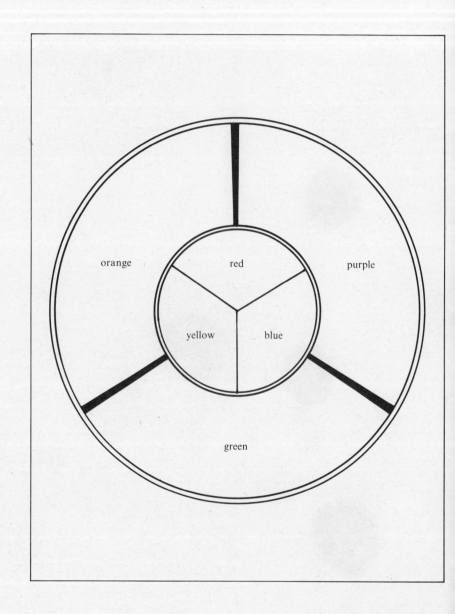

62 A child's drawing.
This sort of drawing could easily be
transferred to embroidery linen for
the child to embroider, using simple
stitches

43

63 *Animal made by a child, who
took her own drawing as a pattern.
She used scraps of woollen fabric,
fur, wool threads and beads to make
an imaginary animal*

Appliqué

Appliqué consists of patches of material laid on to a fabric base and sewn down in one of a number of different ways. If the article being made is of a purely decorative nature, and will not therefore be laundered, the choice of stitches is wide, and the edges of the patches may even be frayed out to give a freer effect. Following are some suggestion of how a circular patch might be sewn down.

A line of running stitch just inside the patch and another just outside it can be linked with a thread in zig-zag fashion, protecting the edge of the patch while making a decoration. Or the circular shapes can be emphasised by working bands of stitches round them. Experiments can be made with varying length of stitches, with working rows of stitches closer or farther apart and so on.

Colour, too, must be considered, in order to show up the applied shapes to advantage and a subtle effect be achieved as follows. On a background of, say, green, with patches in blue, a shaded thread, changing from green to blue, could be used to sew the patches down. A contrasting colour can be introduced, even a metallic thread, but this should be done with discretion or the result will be overpowering. Many different textured threads can be incorporated, from smooth, fine cottons and linens to knobbly knitting yarns. The latter would have to be couched down, being unsuitable for ordinary sewing.

Traditionally, appliqué patches were sewn down with an edging of neat, close blanket stitch, and this is good for laundering purposes, although it does give a rather heavy, solid outline to the shapes. If the article is purely for decoration then the blanket stitching may be varied, by spacing it out or changing the length of the stitches.

Blanket stitch can also be used to make an open filling which lies on top of the fabric. This is done by working the first row into the material and consequent rows into the loops of the previous row, but without piercing the fabric. The last row is again worked through the fabric, anchoring the mesh-like structure top and bottom. This filling stitch can be used to cover an applied patch completely, anchoring it down and protecting the raw edges at the same time. This method can be used when fine pointed shapes are required which would be impossible to cut out in a fraying fabric. Counted thread stitches, such as cross stitch do not combine well with appliqué.

Having learned how to apply the patches, the design of a wall hanging incorporating appliqué could now be considered, keeping in mind the following points. There should be a focal point to the design, one area being accentuated, or the overall effect would be monotonous. At the same time a certain unity should be preserved, this being achieved possibly by having one line running through the whole composition. Consideration should be given to the relative weight of lines in the composition and to the balance between lines and solid forms. It is advisable to stand back from the work at regular intervals, as faults which are not apparent at close range become obvious when seen from a distance.

Felt appliqué

Felt is quite unlike a woven cloth in that it is composed of compressed fibres, and therefore has no warp or weft. This makes it completely different to handle from a normal woven fabric, its main advantage being that it cannot fray. This quality can be fully exploited when using felt for appliqué as fine pointed shapes

*64 Spanish traditional costume
(copyright of the Spanish Bureau
for tourism).*
*This costume looks very complica-
ted to make, but is in fact a clever
arrangement of motifs. The black
strips on the white background and
the light strips on the dark background of the apron could very
easily be worked in appliqué*

65 *Letters, group work in a school.*
For the opening of the new school
building the teachers and pupils
made a wall hanging depicting the
letter combination of HAVO,
MAVO and LEAO (the various
categories of the Dutch school).
A Mexican appliqué technique
using three colours was used for
each letter form

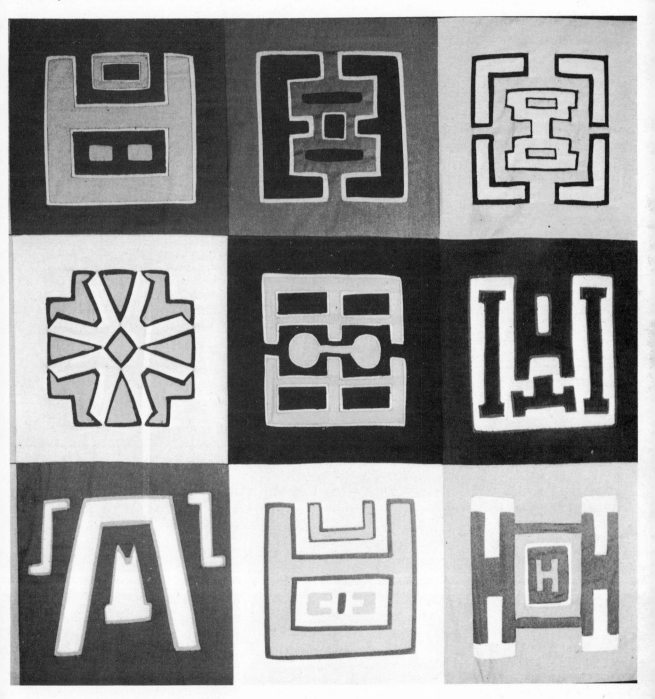

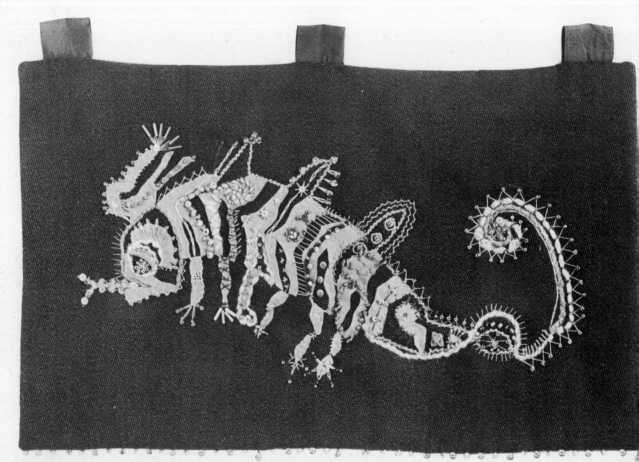

66 *Felt appliqué wall hanging.*
The figure was first cut out of felt,
in one piece, then cut into smaller
pieces which were arranged on the
background, leaving spaces between
them. The pieces were sewn on
using simple embroidery stitches
without covering the crisp edges of
the felt. Beads were added to
complete the design.

Colour plate 5 Soft patchwork.
Several squares are raised up from
the design, adding a three-dimen-
sional element

Colour plate 6 Masks.
Two pieces of material sewn together to make a three-dimensional
shape. Before being stuffed through
the back, the masks were decorated
with embroidery and beads. Details
were added in macramé and bead-
work

and unblurred edges are possible. Several different coloured layers of felt can be tacked together and holes cut back to the various levels revealing the different colours. The shapes thus made can be embellished with embroidery stitches. Felt flower shapes could be cut out and applied to a fabric background for, say, a cushion.

Net appliqué
Net looks delicate, but is, in fact, quite strong and can be used for appliqué in one of two ways. Either the entire background fabric can be covered with net in a contrasting colour and shapes cut out to reveal the background; or net shapes can be cut out and applied to the background in the normal way. Fine stitches should be used, in keeping with the nature of the fabric. Net applied on net gives a delicate lace-like effect.

Machine appliqué
Patches applied by machine are strong, hard wearing and quick to do, and therefore suitable for initials or motifs on children's garments. Zig-zag and automatic stitches, although not essential, do give great scope for a variety of decorative treatments.

Thread appliqué (couching)
Bundles of threads or single threads can be laid on a background and couched down with a plain or decorative stitch. Bundles can be sewn down as they are, or pulled apart into smaller bundles to vary the effect. Threads can also be plaited or knotted before being couched in place.

Another variation is to weave threads through holes made in the ground fabric. Different effects can be obtained by changing the spacing between the couching stitches, covering the laid thread completely in places, spreading the stitches out to reveal it in others. Knobbly knitting wools, weaving gimps, rope and string can all be used to give interesting textures, and the contrast of thick and thin lines, rough and smooth should always be borne in mind.

Braid appliqué
Sewing on braids is a quick way of achieving a bold decorative effect on a plain background. Any commercial product such as rick-rack, fancy woven braids or ribbons can be used. The edges should always be firmly secured and any additional embroidery restrained, so as not to cover too much of the braid. The sewing machine can be used to attach straight edged braids and ribbons, but fancy braid is best sewn on by hand in a rhythmical line, forming a simple geometric pattern.

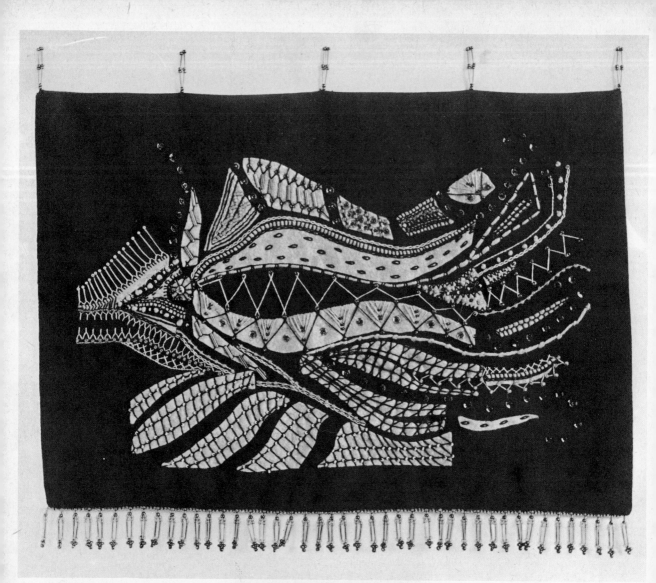

*67 Felt appliqué wall hanging.
A more intricate example of felt
appliqué. The felt shapes have again
been spaced out and embroidery
stitches used to complete the design*

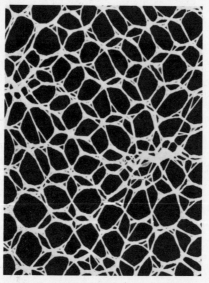

68 Net structure

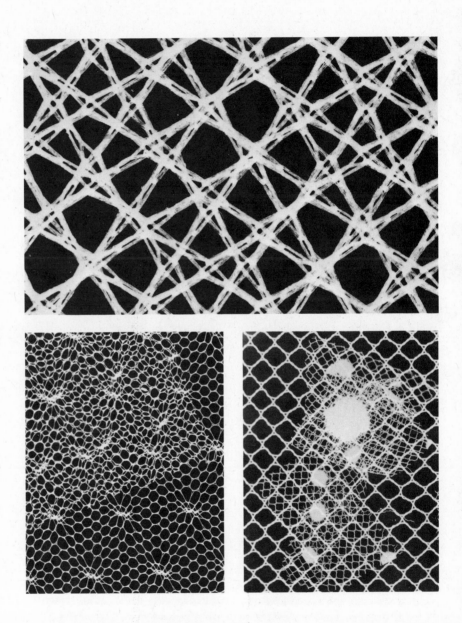

69 Different patterns can be made by placing pieces of net over each other

Net appliqué, simulating a tree. The pattern of net against a dark background is very attractive, and by superimposing layers of net on each other different effects can be created

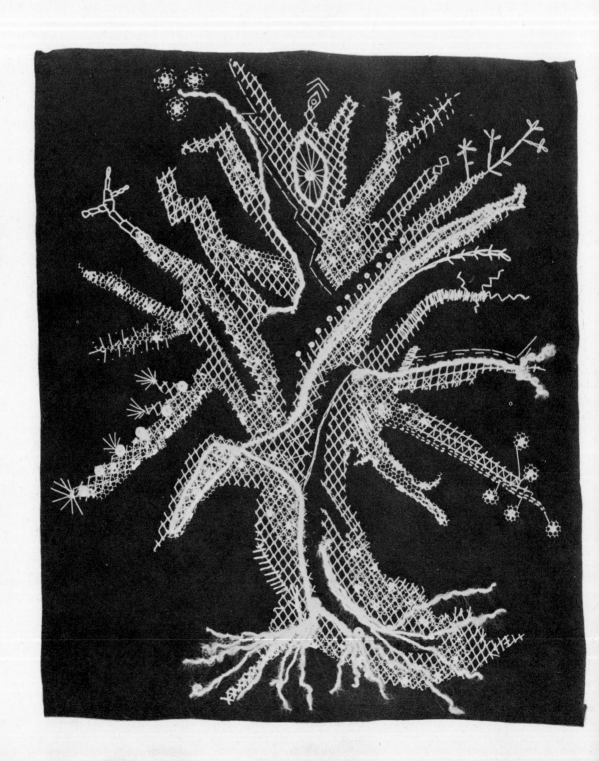

71 Net appliqué in a tree design, with a bead edging

72 Machine appliqué.
This design can be made by sewing together two pieces of contrasting cloth. Cut holes in the top one (the darker), so that the light shows through. Then machine stitch at random using different width, and different length, stitches. Sew on bundles of thread to enhance the design, and fringe the light fabric

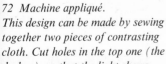

73 Dragon.
This is an imaginary shape made of cloth over cardboard and decorated with couched threads, embroidery stitches and beads. It is stuffed with wadding and has big beads for feet

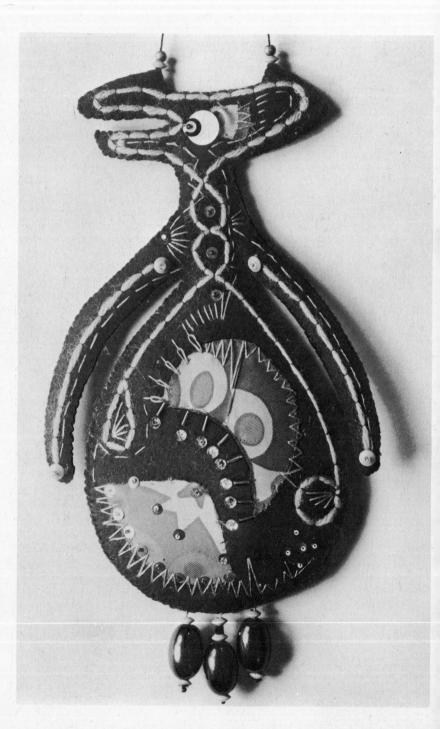

74 Couched threads.
Different kinds of thicknesses of
threads have been couched on to a
coarse background. In some places
the couching stitches are close
together, in others far apart. In
places the threads are sewn on with
embroidery stitches in a rhythmic
pattern

75 Samplers as potholders.
Three different methods have been
used here: the first pair of fish is
mainly decorated with rick-rack
braid; the second pair is decorated
to harmonise with the with the
woven cloth used; the third pair has
a piece of curtain lace sewn completely over the fish shapes to form
a base for the embroidery

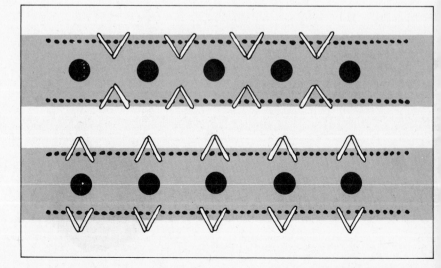

76 Different ways of sewing down
braid.

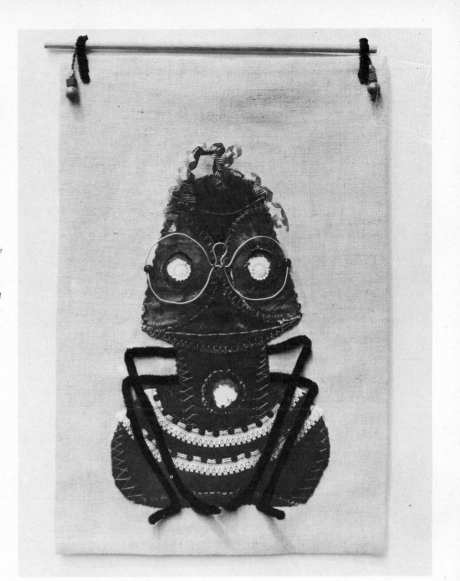

77 Miss Ant.
This is an attractive appliqué con-
structed out of fairly large pieces
of dark fabric on a lighter back-
ground. After placing the main body
shapes, details can be added, in this
case with pieces of lace, braiding,
pipe cleaners, and cellophane ribbon
to accentuate the head

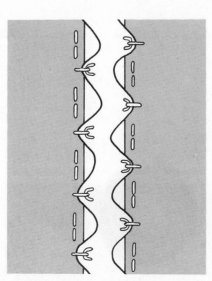

78 A way of sewing down rick-rack
braid

Patchwork

There is a revival of interest in patch-work amongst the young today, and, like knitting and crochet, it is something that can be carried around with one and picked up and worked when time permits. Traditionally, pieced patchwork was made from cotton scraps tacked over card or paper templates, and joined together, in a hexagon, square or other geometric pattern. Pentagonal (five-sided) patches can be joined together to form solid three-dimensional figures. Such a shape, made up in felt, with a bell inside would make a toy for a young baby.

The paper or card templates are cut from a master template in wood or metal. Metal templates can be bought in a wide range of shapes and sizes, but if a particular shape is unobtainable it can be constructed with mathematical instruments and cut out in strong card. Great care must be taken to construct the template accurately, or the whole patchwork pattern will be thrown out. The method for making up patchwork is as follows. From the master template cut out carefully as many paper or thin card templates as will be required. To prepare each patch pin a paper template in place on the wrong side of the fabric and cut out allowing a 7 mm ($\frac{1}{4}$ in.) turning all round. Fold this allowance over the edge of the template and tack through the paper or card. Join the patches together by oversewing on the back or with 'farmer's stitch'. This is a combination of a backstitch and a half cross and is shown in figure 79. When the work is complete take out the tacking stitches and remove the template. The work should be backed and may also be interlined with a synthetic wadding and quilted, making it suitable for bed covers or warm garments.

The design can be carefully worked out beforehand to use specially selected

materials or patches can be covered at random and the pattern built up after-wards. In either case, once the design is planned, it is advisable to number the patches on the back to facilitate putting the work together.

Patterned fabrics require special consideration. Motifs such as flowers or spots can be isolated on a patch and these patches combined with plain ones to form a pattern. Or striped fabrics can be arranged in such a way that interesting geometric and optical designs are formed.

Freestanding patchwork

Patchwork can be used, as has been mentioned, for freestanding, three-dimensional objects, for example a Chinese lantern. Use pentagonal templates, cutting them in card and leaving them in the finished work to give body to the lantern. Other geometric shapes such as the circle, the stripe and the trapezium can also be used to build up an object in the round. When making lampshades occasionally a patch can be missed out, making a hole in the work through which the light will shine. These holes can be decorated with beads either strung across or suspended on a thread within the hole. If glass beads are used rather than wooden or plastic ones the light from the lamp should filter through attractively. It is important that the lamp shade be made big enough to accommodate a bulb without burning the fabric. All patchwork should be lined for a good finish.

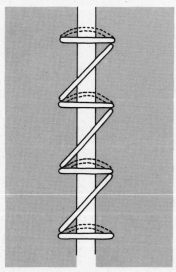

79 Stitch for joining patchwork pieces ('farmer's stitch')

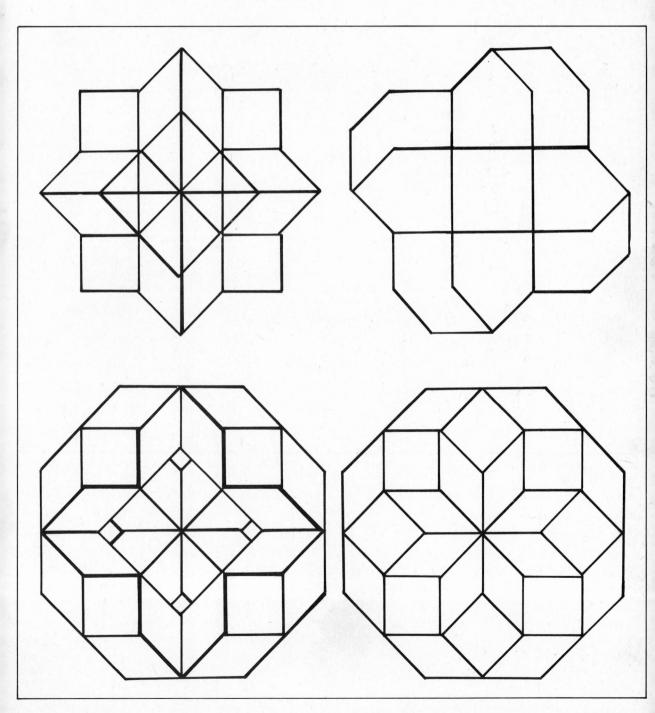

81 Patchwork lampshade.
Pieces of card have been covered
with fabric and joined together,
leaving spaces through which the
light will shine

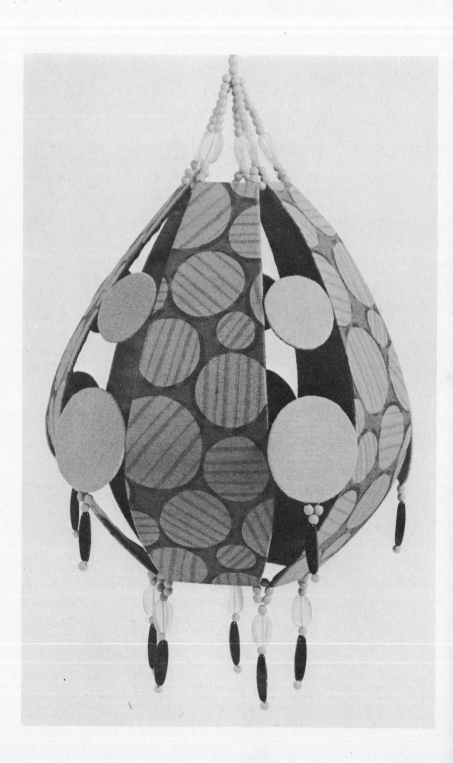

82 Covered box.
This is worked in patchwork over a
round cardboard box. The design
was based on the geometrical print
of the cloth used and the lines of
the box. The lid was stuffed and
covered for a seat

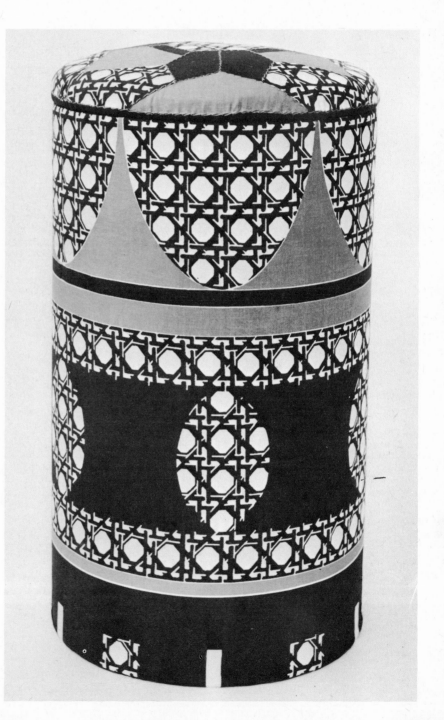

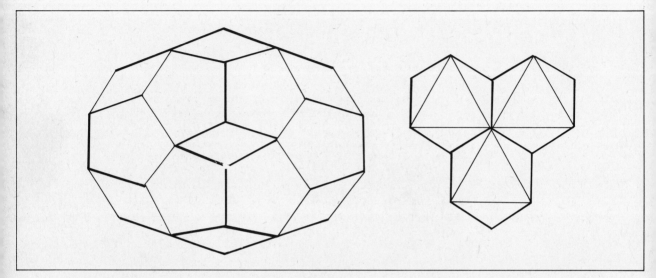

83 Patchwork designs

Webbing and
needlepoint lace

Webbing

The term 'webbing' is used to describe work in threads, stretched across a wooden or metal frame to give a 'spider's web' effect. The frame can be of any shape, but a circular one gives the greatest strength. Warp threads can be attached to the frame by binding or by working a few blanket stitches. In fact, if the frame is of metal, and slippery, it might be advisable to cover the whole thing with blanket stitches before starting work, giving a firm foundation on to which to anchor the warp threads. The basic warp can be embellished in a number of ways. If solid shapes are planned in the design, lay the frame, with the warp prepared, on top of a board. Position the solid patches on the board and pin in place. Attach the patches to the frame and to each other, using long, strong threads. Remove the pins and lift the frame off the board. The work on the frame now forms a basis for embellishment with various techniques.

Knitted patches are particularly suitable for this kind of work as they stretch horizontally and vertically. By pulling on the patches and distorting the knit interesting and unusual shapes can be created. Crochet too, has the same properties, and where crochet squares are incorporated the warp threads could consist of crocheted chains, lending a unity to the work as a whole. Similarly, if the frame is covered with blanket stitches, the threads could be strengthened and made more interesting by being covered in the same way.

The applied patches need not be flat. They can be made of double fabric and stuffed with wadding to give a rounded effect (figure 84).

Needlepoint lace

One of the techniques which naturally springs to mind for the decoration of webbing is that of needlepoint lace. This is basically a structure composed of rows of blanket or buttonhole stitches worked one into the other, giving an elastic net like fabric. The stitches should be made loosely so that the work can be easily stretched within the frame (figure 86). This base can be further decorated with beads or cork balls. Webbing must be worked across an open space, but the frame can be replaced by holes in a piece of fabric, over which threads are stretched and decorated as before.

With this technique the following points should be borne in mind. Threads of an elastic nature such as wool are more suitable than cotton or string which do not 'give'. Some man-made fibres give good results; which these are will have to be decided by trial and error. The fewer the joins in the threads, the more attractive the finished work will look. As it is difficult to manipulate long pieces of thread, the use of a tatting shuttle (for fine threads) or a netting gauge (for coarse threads) is advised. These two traditional gadgets enable the thread to be easily handled without fear of it becoming unwound as happens with a ball or skein.

Children enjoy the webbing technique and it is a good way of using small scraps of knitting or crochet which they may have produced which are useless for any other purpose.

Three-dimensional structures

Three-dimensional shapes can also be made with a flat piece of cork and three wires of 2 mm ($\frac{1}{12}$ in.) diameter (always use the tempered kind). These wires are bent into shape and this should be done carefully, otherwise a kink will appear in the wire and most of the tension will go as well. Make small holes with an

*84 Webbing design containing
elliptical stuffed shapes which were
sewn by machine and decorated with
hand embroidery. Needle lace has
been worked into the large spaces
in a free way to join the small
cushions*

Colour plate 7 Two knitted creatures.

The bird on the right has a main body of knitted purple and black wool. This was an exercise in increasing and decreasing in knitting. A few stitches were cast on and increased until the widest part was reached, then a few rows knitted before beginning the decreasing. Two such pieces were sewn together as illustrated to form the body which was afterwards stuffed, leaving the non-stuffed areas as wings. A fringe was attached to part of the wings. The legs are simply chenille covered wire, pushed into the body up to the neck. The head is of knitted black wool and the beak of felt. Eyes, nose and tongue are beads.

The small cat-like figure was knitted almost as a triangle, sewed up the back and stuffed. The head is of a pink knitted wool, the legs and tail, pushed through the body, are chenille wire, and the features are added in buttons

Colour plate 8 Embroidered wall hanging.

The designer of this wall hanging based the design on 'earth' and made the centre of leather and the outer 'moon glow' of batik cloth. The 'earth' was covered with various earth-coloured threads depicting land, some reaching out to the atmosphere. The surrounding area was embroidered to depict the sun, moon and sky

85 Metal frame nailed to a board
while appliqué patches are incorporated into the work

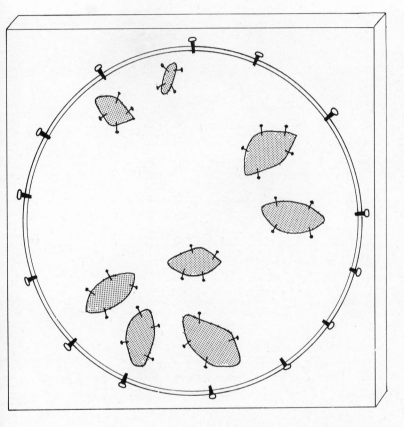

upward slant in the sides of the cork
with a pair of scissors, and push the
wires in. If the holes are made on the
top of the cork, the wires will probably
jump out again.

The wires should be bent into rhythmical shapes, and it is important to be
aware always of the spaces between the
wires as well as the shapes of the wires
themselves. Stretch threads between the
wires to make a spatial design (see figure
88). To prevent the threads slipping, the
wires can be covered before bending
with blanket stitch. Or, make a crochet
chain and pass the wire through it.
Great variety can be obtained by working with different thicknesses of thread,
applying needlepoint lace and adding
beads.

87 Lace parasol formerly owned by Queen Emma of the Netherlands (copyright Rijksmuseum, Amsterdam). It was made in Nanduti-lace technique, in Paraguay

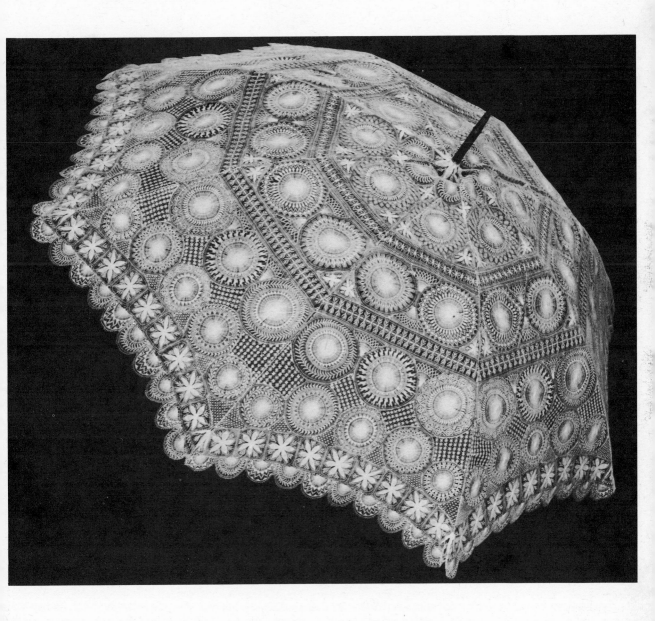

88 *Webbing design with a cork base.*
Three wires were bent into the desired shape and pushed into a cork base. Then threads were stretched between them, making an interesting spatial design. The beads were strung onto the wires before the wires were bent into shape and were secured with blanket stitches

89 Hanging decoration.
A few curtain rings were covered in
crochet and incorporated into a
design with stretched warp, needleweaving and needlepoint lace

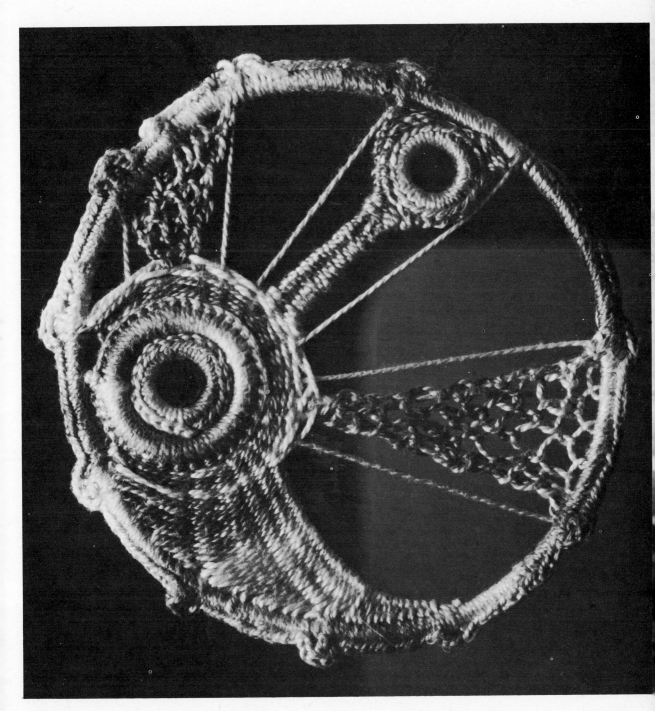

Macramé

Macramé is a multiple thread technique by which a fabric can be constructed. Children should learn it before knitting or crochet as it teaches co-ordination of the fingers, and is quick and easy to master. The basic knots are the square knot (also known as the flat knot), the half knot, the clove hitch (cording) and the Josephine knot.

Any firm rounded thread is suitable for knotting, for instance twine, thick wool, tubular nylon, piping cord, or rope. The threads must be cut long enough to complete the piece of work as joins are unsatisfactory. The more complex the design the more thread will be taken up in the working. For a simple design cut all threads six times the desired length of the work, plus 500 mm (20 in.) extra. For example, for an article which is to measure 500 mm (20 in.) when finished each thread must by cut 6×500 mm (20 in.) plus 500 mm (20 in.) which equals 3·5 m (11 ft 10 in.). This looks long but is immediately halved when the threads are set on.

Setting on can be done in two ways which are clearly shown in figures 95 and 96. The foundation cord should be stretched taut while the work is in progress, and suggestions for ways of achieving this are shown in figure 97. These include using a board with nails, table clamps, the back of a chair, and coat hooks. Work can also be attached to a board with sticking plaster or tape.

To learn the basic knots tie a foundation cord tightly between two points and set a number of threads on to it. Begin with the half knot, which can be worked to the right and to the left (figures 90a–c). These two movements worked in sequence form the square knot. A series of half knots will twist like a barley sugar stick, but a series of square knots makes a flat braid. Only the right and left hand threads are actually knotted – the two central threads act as an anchor round which the knots are made. The knots can be moved up on this anchor thread, to form picots on the edges, and beads can be slipped on to it, adding richness to the work. When working in square or half knots the threads should be set on in multiples of four. A fabric can be formed by taking two threads from one square or half knot and two from its neighbour across alternate rows, thus linking the knots together. Balls can be made on a square knot braid or fabric in the following way. Work, say, seven square knots and roll them up, threading the anchor threads through to the back of the work above the first knot. The next square knot worked will hold this 'ball' in position.

The vertical clove hitch is shown in figure 92. It is worked on two threads, one acting as an anchor and one as the knotting thread. The movement can be followed from the diagram. The horizontal clove hitch can be worked on any number of threads. One, either the extreme right hand or extreme left hand thread acts as an an anchor and the other threads are knotted over it as shown in figure 93. Clove hitches can also be knotted round a diagonal thread to form diamond patterns (figure 100). Several rows of horizontal clove hitches form a very solid structure and are useful when making free standing three-dimensional objects.

The Josephine knot (figures 91a and b) is actually a braiding knot and looks better worked fairly loosely. It can be worked with multiple threads on either side instead of the single threads as shown in the diagram. This makes for a very decorative, ornate knot.

It is advisable for the beginner to work in one colour only. Macramé is

90 a. The half knot (twist to the right)
b. The half knot (twist to the left)
c. The square knot (combination of a and b)
91 Josephine knot.
a. Make a loop in the left hand cord in an anti-clockwise direction.
Make a similar knot with the right hand cord but in a clockwise direction, interlacing it with the first loop in an over-under-over-under sequence
b. Pull evenly and begin loop for next knot
92 Vertical clove hitch
93 Horizontal clove hitch

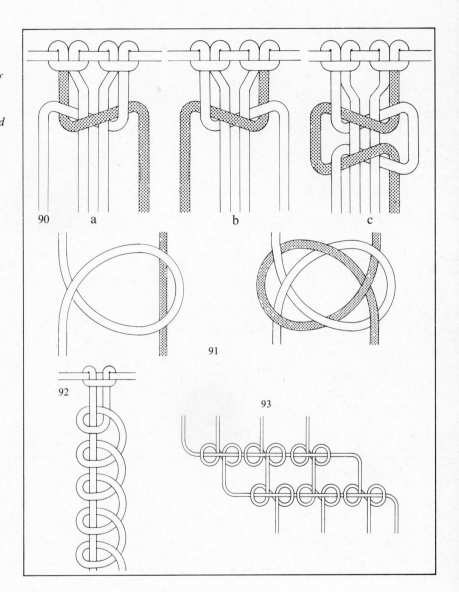

94 How to measure thread for macramé

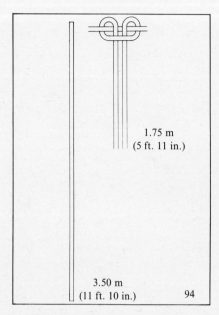

1.75 m
(5 ft. 11 in.)

3.50 m
(11 ft. 10 in.)   94

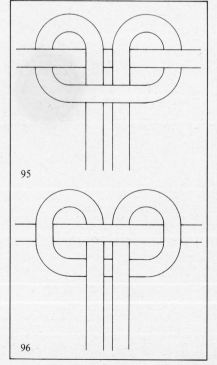

95

96

95 Setting on, front view
96 Setting on, back view

most often worked in a natural colour twine and this shows up the knots to their full advantage. Colour, unless very skillfully used can confuse the appearance of the work, and should only be introduced when the knotting technique is thoroughly mastered. The introduction of colour is most effective when using the clove hitch, as any thread being used as an anchor thread is completely hidden by the clove hitches, to emerge eventually at some different point in the design. In this way colours can be 'moved' across the design with interesting results.

The ways of finishing off macramé knotting vary with each individual piece of work, but the two most common methods are to end with a knotted fringe, which can be trimmed to the required length; or to work a few rows of clove hitches, darn the ends back, trim and secure with a spot of glue.

Macramé can be worked flat or freestanding. For the latter the threads used must be sufficiently firm and the knots worked close enough together to make the work stand. This does not apply, of course, to articles such as lampshades which have a supporting metal frame.

Free design

Below are some suggestions for free experimentation with macramé. Try using wires instead of threads as anchors for square knots and clove hitches. When the knotting is complete the wires can be bent into any shape and joined to each other with further knots. Bundles of wire can be covered and opened out into fantastic compositions, the ends of the knotting threads being fringed or fluffed out for further interest.

Freestanding forms need not be regular in shape. Extra threads can be inserted

between knots to increase the volume and bundles of threads can be tied together to decrease it.

Combination of macramé with other techniques

Knotting can be incorporated successfully into other kinds of work. For example macramé can be used for hair or beards on dolls and puppets, or as a finish on clothing or wall decorations. Where material allows, the weft threads can be withdrawn at the bottom of a garment or hanging and the remaining warp threads knotted into a decorative fringe.

98 Detail of the wall decoration called Castle in the Air.
In this design thick and thin sisal was used, and many of the knots stand out in relief on the surface of the work

99 Macramé mask.
This is a three-dimensional mask made with macramé, using different knots. The raised shapes for the eye and on the head and hanging on the ears are prepared potatoes. Fluffed out fringes form the beard and hair-like decorations. Beads were also added for teeth and eyes and for the earrings

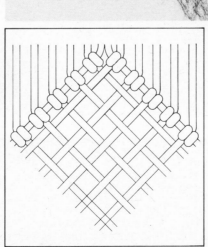

100 Diamond patterned braid work incorporated in macramé

101 Macramé tree.
Three wires were bent to form the
trunk, and joined together by knott-
ing the threads from one to the
threads of its neighbour. The bran-
ches were then bent into shape and
finished off with frayed out threads
and beads

Creative knitting and crochet

New ways in knitting

Knitting and crochet are techniques from which fabric can be constructed. Knitting, because of the way the loops are linked laterally and vertically, has two particular qualities. Firstly, if a stitch is dropped off the needle, then the stitch below it drops also and so on until a ladder or run is formed. Secondly, a piece of knitted fabric can be divided in two by pulling out one horizontal thread. Both these qualities can be used creatively. A stitch can be dropped on purpose and the horizontal bars in the resulting ladder woven into with a braid or crochet chain; or the ladder can simply be left to make an open space in the design. Beads can be used to decorate the spaces, and can also be knitted into the fabric in the first place. To do this the beads are strung on to the yarn before the knitting is begun and a bead moved up into place when needed. This is normally done between two pearl stitches (figure 102). Two beads would lie between three pearl stitches and so on. In stocking stitch (one row plain, one row pearl), the beads would lie on the back of the work.

The stretchable quality of knitting can be exploited to the full in the webbing technique described earlier, often in combination with weaving (in the ladders), needlepoint lace, beading and decorative stitchery. A ladder may be stopped at any point, giving alternate open and closed areas.

When knitting is divided by pulling out a horizontal thread a looped edge results, which can be used to attach the work to a frame for webbing, or as a basis for further stitching, or for macramé.

Interesting effects can be created by changing the sizes of the needles during knitting, resulting in stitches which vary in scale; or by casting stitches on and off at random to give an irregular outer shape; and by changing the colours of the wool during work.

New ways in crochet

Crochet, like knitting can be worked irregularly to give freer results, and crochet chains and cords can be specially prepared to be incorporated into weaving (as a warp or weft threads); into embroidery (couched); and into webbing and braiding.

Freestanding designs

Both knitting and crochet can be used in the construction of work in the round. A number of knitted or crocheted pieces can be sewn up and stuffed to make toy animals or just decorative shapes. Knitted or crocheted loops give extra volume and textural interest to a design (figure 106). Spacial compositions can be evolved on a frame, using knitting and crochet combined with webbing.

Use up any scraps of knitting or crochet, sewing them together and stuffing them. The resulting form, however fanciful, could become the starting point for the design of an animal or doll.

102 The beads are positioned in the connecting loops in between two pearl stitches

This is an example of what can
be achieved in creative knitting.
The designer worked with thin
needles and woollen thread, varying
the thicknesses and creating a thick
and thin design. The knitted piece
was then stretched and secured
inside a frame and decorated spar-
ingly with beads

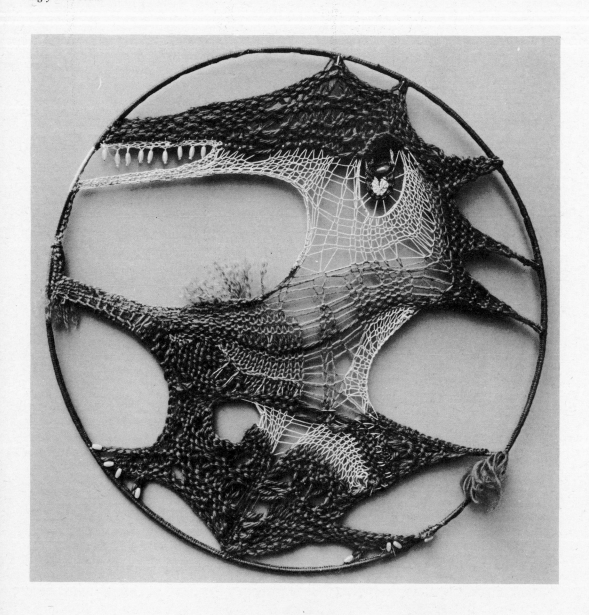

104 Chicken.
Individual pieces such as for the head were first made, then joined together with threads connected to the wire frame

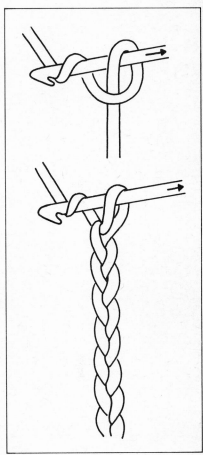

105 Crocheting a chain with crochet hook

*106 Animal made of looped crochet.
The looped crochet was worked
from a covered ring at the base of
the figure, using a double thread in
two shades of the same colour. The
neck was made by decreasing the
number of stitches. A bead was used
for the eye and the beak was lined
with felt*

107 Wobbles.
These are easily made using curtain
rings covered with crochet, cork
balls, thin wire and a cork base,
with a board glued underneath for
added stability

Three-dimensional shapes

All the techniques previously discussed in this book can be used to make three-dimensional shapes. These require careful planning and a thorough understanding of the materials being used. Making up one or two three-dimensional objects such as dolls would give experience in handling different materials, and in planning 'in the round'.

'Mosaic' for a hanging doll

Take a piece of paper 300 mm × 400 mm (12 in. × 16 in.) and fold it in half. On this draw one line, straight or curved from one edge of the paper to the other. Draw up to four more lines in any position (figure 109). Cut out along the lines, spread out the 'mosaic' pieces to form a design (in this case a doll shape). Lay the pieces on to fabric and chalk round each shape. Cut out, leaving a seam allowance. Transfer these pieces on to another fabric, in a contrasting colour and pin them to it, right sides facing. Tack the two layers together and machine round each piece, leaving a small gap as an opening. Cut out each shape, turn it inside out and stuff, closing up the gap with neat oversewing. Decorate these stuffed shapes with any suitable technique, for instance, appliqué, surface stitchery, beading, or a combination of all three. Or sew on found objects such as bottletops, corks, curtain rings, metal chains or buttons.

When the pieces have been suitably decorated join them together with string, beads, crochet chains, plaiting or knotting. This should be done loosely enough for the parts to swing in relation to each other.

Make the hair from wool, raw wool, nylon stockings or feathers. Almost any scrap materials can be incorporated into this kind of doll.

Dolls and animals

Make a doll, following the instructions in figure 114. This is intended to be a basic pattern, which can be adapted to make a doll to play with or one purely for decoration. The size of the head may seem overlarge, but this is necessary to give the finished doll a well-proportioned appearance. The two dolls in figure 113 are made from the basic pattern.

Other suggestions for stuffed figures include floppy dolls, hand puppets, golliwogs and animals. The animals, which can be toys or decorations, need not be realistic, but can evolve from the designer's imagination like the three headed beast illustrated in figure 110. Patterned fabrics, scraps of fur, knotted or knitted pieces could all be incorporated with amusing results.

108 Cat shape.
Draw out the design on paper, and
cut out pattern pieces. Place these
on double fabric and cut round.
Tack like shapes together, right
sides facing and sew round, leaving
a small gap. Turn inside out, stuff
and close gap. Join the stuffed
patches together loosely, and decor-
ate with beads, embroidery, crochet,
or knitting. The backs and fronts of
the patches can have different
decorative treatments

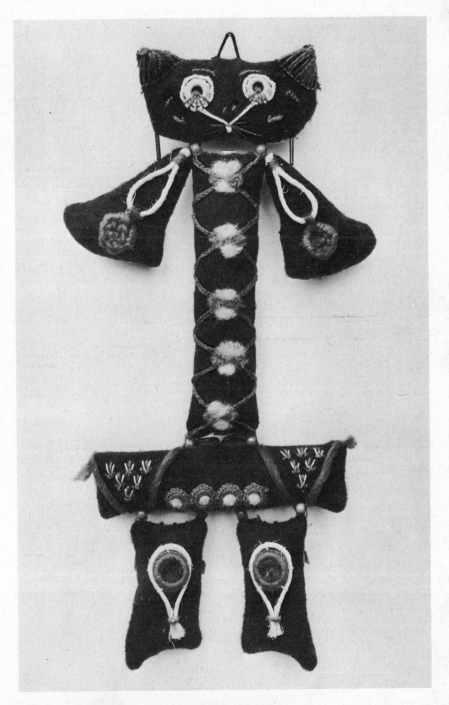

109 Two doll shapes from the
same basic 'mosaic'

110 Three-headed beast.
This was made more like a con-
ventional stuffed toy, except for the
very wide body which has to accommodate three identical necks and
heads. The material was chosen for
its particular texture, and with three
heads already the animal needs little
further decoration except for bead
eyes and tiny beads for teeth

111 Mascot.
Two pieces of cloth were laid on top
of each other and the shape of the
head outlined in chalk. The pieces
were tacked together and then
machine sewn, leaving an open space
at the top of the head for stuffing.
Then the shape was cut out and
resewn with a close zig-zag machine
stitch, stuffed, and the hole sewn up.
The eyes and decorations were then
applied on to the face, beads added,
and hair made of knotted or tangled
wool

112 Animal figure.
The basic shape was first machine
sewn, right sides facing, then turned
out and stuffed. Features were
applied using decorative stitches.
Couched threads and tassels were
added

113 These dolls were made according to the patterns on the following
pages

114 Doll pattern

1. The doll's head (A) can be any size, but the rest of the measurements must correspond in size. The body (B) must be as wide as the head and 1½ times as long

2. The leg (C) must be 1½ times the body in length, and can be cut straight or shaped, depending on the kind of doll

3. The arm (D) to the wrist should be the same length as the body, and the hand half the length of the upper leg

4. A bent wire (E) should be used inside the doll to prevent the neck flopping

5. The neck is pushed inside the body to make a filling tube through which the stuffing and wire are inserted

6. The head goes over the wire and the two neck tubes are sewn together

The doll's head can be made in different ways. For instance, a flat head can be made by putting a gusset between front and back parts; or the head can be cut in profile.

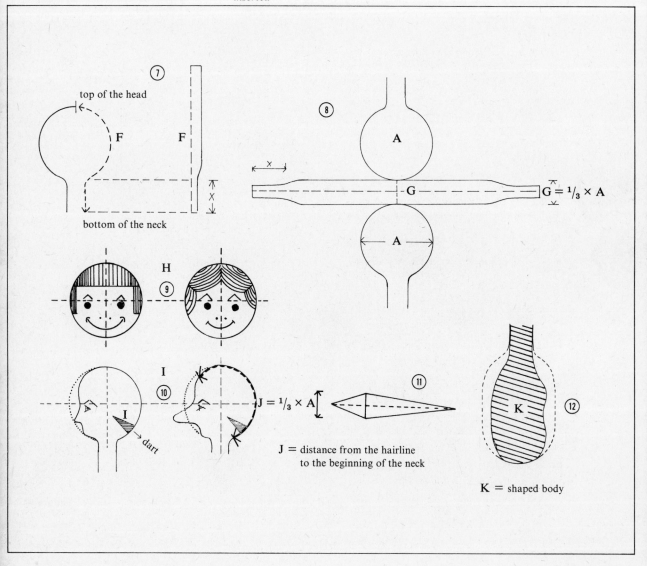

7. To determine length of gusset (F):
X = length of neck, F = length of strip
8. How to make up the head (G)
9. How to embroider the face (H)
10. Two ways to form a profile (I). Notice the dart for giving the cheek shape on the left hand figure. In the other figure, that of a clown, an extra gusset is inserted between the two Xs

11. The shape and the length of the gusset for the profile head
12. The body can be shaped as illustrated (K)
The pattern pieces should be cut as follows:
2 pieces for head (A)
2 pieces for body (B)
4 pieces for leg (C)
4 pieces for arm (D)

1 gusset for head (G)
or 1 gusset for profile head (J)

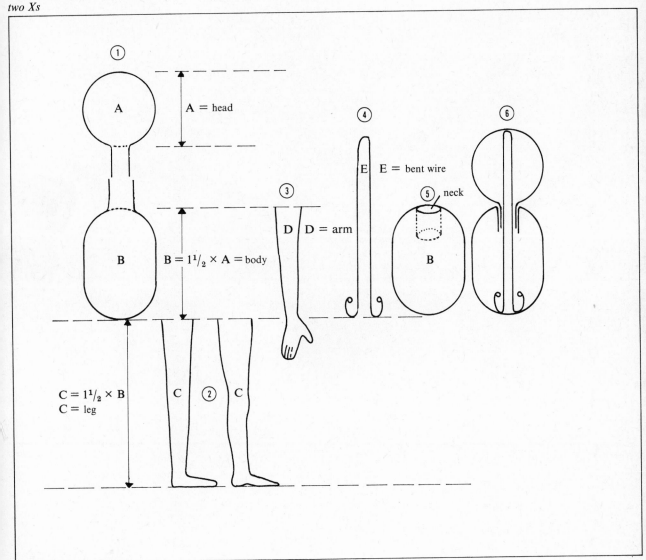

115 This fly was made basically of
wire, completely covered with
macramé knots worked in different
sorts of woollen threads. Other
wires were attached to the first and
covered with threads, in crochet and
a combination of other techniques

116 Mask.
The basic form was made of papier mâché on which the shape was stretched. The material is a coarse sack cloth, and was pulled and pushed into shape and invisibly stitched. The eyes are wool strands tacked in place, and the hair was made of bunches of thread roughly sewn on. Stuffing must be loose or the face shape would be distorted

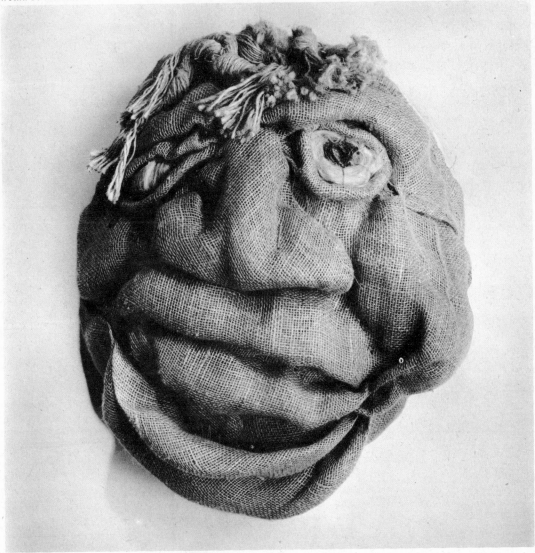

Using unusual materials

Apart from the wide range of fabrics which can be bought, it is possible to create one's own colours and patterns with the use of dyes.

Dyeing materials

If a fabric in the colour of one's choice is not available, it is a simple matter, following the manufacturer's instructions, to dye cloth at home quite successfully. Dyes come in liquid or powder form, for cold and hot water dyeing.

Making patterns on cloth

Children like to paint directly on to fabric with dyes. The design can be faintly marked out in pencil, the dyes applied with a brush, and when dry the pattern can be further embellished with embroidery or appliqué patches. The latter could also be dyed to fit the design.

Tie and dye

Another satisfying way of decorating cloth is to tie it in little 'doughnut' shape bundles with string or rubber bands and then immerse it in a dye bath. When the fabric has been removed and is almost dry the string or rubber bands should be removed and the fabric ironed. This removes the creases and sets the colour. The areas of cloth which were covered by the string or rubber bands will have resisted the dye and a pattern of roughly circular shapes in the original colour of the cloth is produced.

Dying other materials

Threads can be dyed for projects, also flax and wool in their raw state. Care must be taken to removed all traces of oil from the wool or the colours will not permeate the fibre.

Beans, dried peas, melon seeds, fruit stones and pips all take dye well. Beans and peas must be dyed with cold water or they will swell and begin to cook, making them useless to work with. Apart from commercially produced dyes it is possible to make one's own from natural substances.

Red wine, spinach water, red cabbage water, strong cold tea, blackberry and blackcurrant juice all give satisfactory results. Inks can also be used, although Indian ink should be avoided as it is not fast.

Beans, pips and pieces of potato can be used as beads and can be coloured by immersing in a dye bath for twelve to twenty-four hours depending on the absorbency of the substances being dyed. A glass or earthenware pot should be used as a container. Tin should be avoided as it would rust and contaminate the dye. The beans are removed from the dye bath when ready and rinsed under cold water until the water runs clear. They can be patted dry on kitchen paper and should be strung immediately, using a needle with a large eye and strong thread. The end of the thread is knotted and the 'beads' are pierced centrally with the needle and pushed down along the thread towards the knot. The completed string should be hung in an airy place to dry out. This may take several days, and the beads should be moved on the string periodically to prevent them sticking together. Once the beads are dry the colour may be deepened by spraying with sun-tanning and when that is absorbed, with hair laquer.

Potato dyeing

It is best to use potatoes which have been grown in a clay rather than a sandy soil, as sand grown potatoes tend to be brittle when dry, making them unsuitable for beads or even for larger work. Cut the potatoes into even sized bead shapes, remembering that they will shrink con-

117 Dyed cloth sampler.
The patches can be painted on with
ink or textile dye. After drying the
cloth thoroughly, it was stretched
on a frame and embroidered with a
variety of stitches to emphasise the
design

siderably when dry. Dry out the potato 'beads' for an hour in the air, then immerse in the dye bath for one or two hours. Remove them and string carefully on skewers to dry. At this stage their appearance will not be very attractive, but will improve with drying. This should be done in a cool place as too much warmth will cause mold to form. Like the beans, the potato beads can be given a finish with a coat of varnish or laquer.

Whole potatoes can be sculpted with the aid of an apple corer and a potato peeler, and afterwards dyed. The miniature 'sculptures' should be dried in a cool place and varnished.

The dye bath

For lighter tones less dye powder is required than for deeper tones, and the objects being dyed can be left in the bath for a shorter period. The final colour of natural objects such as beans depends largely on the original skin colour, so a mixture of different types of beans in one dye bath will result in an interesting range of colours and tones.

If a particular colour is not available dye colours can be mixed on the same principle as mixing paints.

Fabric strips

Long strips of fabric can be cut or torn for use in knitting, crochet, as warp or weft threads in weaving or as hair for dolls.

Natural materials and discarded objects

Natural materials such as grasses can be used as a basis for weaving into mats or cloth; shells, twigs and stones combine well with macramé and beads for curtains, and room dividers can be made from rolled strips of paper or wood shavings. All kinds of materials which are discarded in the home can be utilised – for instance bottle tops, egg cartons, buttons, old nylon stockings, metal foil and pieces of wire.

Bibliography

Inspiration for Embroidery, Constance Howard, Batsford, London; Branford, Newton Centre

Design in Embroidery, Kathleen Whyte, Batsford, London; Branford, Newton Centre

Design in Fabric and Thread, Aileen Murray, Studio Vista, London

Creative Thread Design, Mair Morris, Batsford, London; Branford, Newton Centre

Introducing Weaving, Phyl Shillinglaw, Batsford, London

Weaving is for Anyone, Jean Wilson, Van Nostrand Reinhold, London, New York

Introducing Knitting, Audrie Stratford, Batsford, London

Introducing Macramé, Eirian Short, Batsford, London; Watson-Guptill, New York

The Technique of Macramé, Bonny Schmid-Burleson, Batsford, London; Branford, Newton Centre

The Ashley Book of Knots, Clifford Ashley, Faber, London; Doubleday, New York

Needleweaving, Edith John, Batsford, London; Branford, Newton Centre

Simple Stitches, Anne Butler, Batsford, London

Dictionary of Embroidery Stitches, Hodder, London

Appliqué Stitchery, Jean Ray Laury, Van Nostrand Reinhold, London, New York

Needle Lace and Needle Weaving, Jill Nordfors, Studio Vista, London; Van Nostrand Reinhold, New York

The Stitches of Creative Embroidery, Jacqueline Enthoven, Van Nostrand Reinhold, London, New York

Macramé, The Art of Creative Knotting, Virginia I. Harvey, Van Nostrand Reinhold, London, New York

The Bead Book, Ida-Merete Erlandsen and Hetty Mooi, Van Nostrand Reinhold, London, New York

Stitchery Art and Craft, Nik Krevitsky, Van Nostrand Reinhold, London, New York

Knit Art, Ferne Cone, Van Nostrand Reinhold, London, New York